MW00388715

AMERICA IN THE BALANCE
God's Perspective on Nations and What to Do

INDIVIDUAL GUIDE

© 2017, 2018 Forerunners of America.
This may be freely reproduced and distributed provided the content is not changed.

Preparing Christians to stand firm now and through difficult times.
Preparing Christians to minister with greater fruitfulness now
and through difficult times.

OUR MESSAGE

We are living in unusual days and believe that greater national challenges likely lie ahead. While this might be unsettling to many, our message is to help people discern the hour and respond in faith, not fear. Indeed, in the midst of tumultuous days, *Forerunners of America* is believing God for the greatest spiritual harvest our nation has seen in generations.

DESIRED OUTCOMES

We desire to see five outcomes wherever our message is presented:

1 A BETTER UNDERSTANDING OF GOD'S "NOW" MESSAGE FOR HIS CHURCH AND OUR NATION
(Jeremiah 23:22; Ezekiel 3:17; Colossians 1:28-29)

2 A GREATER HEART FOR THE LOST AND LEADING PEOPLE TO FAITH IN CHRIST
(Matthew 9:35-37; Luke 19:10; Acts 1:8)

3 UNITY WITHIN THE LOCAL CHURCH AND THROUGHOUT THE BODY OF CHRIST
(John 17:23; 1 Peter 3:8-9; Colossians 3:15)

4 A BALANCE OF GOD'S GRACE AND A HEALTHY FEAR OF THE LORD
(1 Cor. 15:9-10; Psalm 34:7-14; Proverbs 9:10)

5 HEARTS THAT WILL CRY OUT TO GOD FOR MERCY FOR OUR NATION
(Psalm 130:1-8; Zephaniah 2:1-3)

CONTENTS

INTRODUCTION

On the surface, not much has changed. As Americans, we continue to pursue our careers, go shopping, entertain ourselves, and enjoy our favorite coffee. But what if something major has changed? And what if God is trying to draw attention to this change? In this study, we will consider questions such as: "What is God saying to our nation?" "Does God even care about nations today?" "What is our nation's trajectory, and what are the implications?"

America in the Balance aims to answer these questions and many others. God is wonderfully gracious, kind, and loving, but He is also holy and just. How does a biblical understanding of God's holiness and justice inform us of the unusual hour in which we are living? What are the implications of God's justice for nations today—and especially for America?

Throughout this study, it is vital that we understand the macro-picture of nations presented throughout the Bible as we specifically evaluate what is taking place in our nation and what we should do. It is our hope that this study will highlight the serious nature of what is unfolding before us, as well as what this means for us and our loved ones.

One of the rallying cries in *Forerunners of America* is, "Discern the hour and respond in faith, not fear." While our journey might not be easy, let's embrace our reality and respond by trusting our almighty, faithful God. Let's understand what is actually taking place, and then let's believe that God wants to use us in this pivotal moment in our nation's history.

www.ForerunnersOfAmerica.org

HOW TO USE THIS STUDY

This study is designed to guide individuals through a self-discovery process. To facilitate this, each lesson includes a combination of insights, discussion questions, and insight answers to those discussion questions. These answers can be found at the end of each lesson and are an integral element to this study. After answering the questions, users are strongly encouraged to read the provided answers, recognizing that these answers are by no means exclusive or exhaustive. Rather they are intended to serve as additional insights.

This study incorporates a lot of Scripture. For convenience, Scripture references have been set apart in red text. Those references in bold are passages we especially encourage users to look up and read.

The goal of this 10-part study is to help us learn how to stand firm now and through greater difficulties in the future, and to learn how to minister with more fruitfulness now and in the future. The first two lessons focus on biblical principles regarding God's purpose and relationship with nations. The next three lessons evaluate America's relationship with God. And the last five lessons emphasize practical application.

For those who find this study useful, a teacher's guide designed for small groups and church Sunday schools can be freely downloaded at www.ForerunnersOfAmerica.org. It is specifically designed to allow anyone to facilitate group discussion regardless of teaching experience and Bible knowledge. We hope that you will consider facilitating a small group to share this information with your friends and loved ones.

It is our prayer and heart's desire that this study will stimulate sober contemplation regarding God's justice and its implications for nations today. *America in the Balance* is merely a tool intended to facilitate this, and we hope it blesses you!

DOES GOD CARE ABOUT NATIONS TODAY?
(LESSON 1)

Insight:

Two ideological camps seem to dominate our society. The one camp believes that our country is following an upward trajectory. There may be bumps along the way, but overall things are well, and they are destined to improve over time. The other camp is influenced by nearly two decades of terrorism, economic crises, social unrest, geopolitical shifts, and the threat of war, which have produced an apocalyptic atmosphere. This is fueled by the countless dystopian books, movies, and television shows which have flooded the market, and the sense that the American dream is on life support. People in this camp have an innate understanding that something is terribly wrong—that something has changed in our country—and they are seeking answers. But, they are looking in the wrong places.

When we understand what the Bible has to say about God's justice and its implications for nations today, we may find that this apocalyptic sense provides a natural door of opportunity for us to share the gospel. We may also discover a burden to warn those who are overly optimistic. At the very least, we will understand what God is endeavoring to accomplish through times of difficulty. *The goal of this 10-part study is to help us learn how to stand firm now and through greater difficulties in the future, and learn how to minister with more fruitfulness now and in the future.* While some of the content of this study may be discouraging, we can remain encouraged if we stay focused on the bigger picture of God's redemptive purposes.

Insight:

The gospel message is global in scope. The good news is that anyone can participate in the kingdom of God through repentance and faith in Jesus Christ alone (**Matt. 28:18–20**; **John 3:16**; **Rom. 10:8–13**). Our salvation doesn't depend upon:
- whether we are circumcised (**Rom. 3:28–30**; 1 Cor. 7:19; Col. 2:11–14). Circumcision was the Old Testament symbol signifying God's covenant people (Gen. 17:10–11).
- whether we are a Jew or a Gentile (Gal. 3:26–28; **Rom. 3:29–30**).
- whether we adhere to the Law of Moses (Gal. 3:2–12; **Rom. 3:27–28**).
- whether we observe Jewish festivals or keep the Sabbath day (Rom. 14:1–6, 13–14, 17; **Col. 2:16–17, 20–23**).
- whether we eat certain foods or abstain from certain foods (Rom. 14:1–6, 13–14, 17; **Col. 2:16–17, 20–23**).

The gospel message applies to everyone, regardless of their nationality, race, or culture (**John 3:14–18**; 1 John 4:9–16). This fact that the gospel is global in scope raises the question, "Does God still care about nations today?" To answer this question, we first need to consider God's purpose for creating nations.

> **Question 1:** According to **Genesis 11:1–9**, what was God's purpose for dividing the earth into nations?

_____

_____

_____

_____

_____

_____

Question 2: According to Acts 17:24–27, what was God's purpose for dividing the earth into nations?

_____

_____

_____

_____

_____

_____

_____

Question 3: According to 2 Chronicles 15:1–9, how did God accomplish His purpose of using nations to draw people back to Himself?

_____

_____

_____

_____

_____

_____

_____

Question 4: Are you aware of any events in our nation's history which God used to bring people to repentance and to faith in Him?

_____

_____

_____

_____

_____

_____

Insight:
Nations also play an important role in God's long-term redemptive plan. Rather than nations becoming obsolete, when Jesus returns and God redeems His creation, He will also redeem the nations!

Question 5: According to Isaiah 2:3–4, Revelation 21:23–26, and Revelation 22:1–3, what does the Bible teach regarding nations in God's future plan for the earth?

_____

_____

_____

_____

_____

_____

Question 6: In what ways is America helping to draw people back to God?

_____

_____

_____

_____

_____

_____

_____

Insight:

God cares about nations today. Nations serve an important role in God's redemption plan as He uses them to draw people to Himself. But what about those nations who stand in opposition to God? This will be the topic of our next lesson.

Question 7: How has this lesson influenced your thinking?

_____

_____

_____

_____

_____

_____

Prayer Points:

- Ask God to reveal to you specific ways in which we as a nation are both succeeding and failing to help draw people back to God.
- Ask God how you as an American can help draw people back to Him.
- Ask God to give you a greater burden for seeing people come to Him than you have for seeing our nation protected and blessed.

Question 1:
- **Answer:** God divided the earth into nations at the Tower of Babel as an act of judgment. Having recently experienced a global flood designed to cleanse the earth of its wickedness, mankind again acted in rebellion to God and sought to regain what they had lost in the flood. God foiled mankind's plans by confusing the language and dividing them into nations, in hope that mankind would stop rebelling against God (Deut. 32:8).
- **Answer:** God divided people into nations to limit mankind's ability to *collectively* strive against God and His commandments.
- **Answer:** God divided mankind into nations to remind us of our need for Him and to make us more dependent on Him.

Question 2:
- **Answer:** Nations are designed to draw people back to God.

Question 3:
- **Answer:** Through Azariah the prophet, God gave King Asa and all the people of the nation of Judah two promises (verses 1–2 and 7). King Asa and the people believed these promises and acted in faith.
- **Answer:** God troubled the disobedient nation of Judah with every kind of distress and with international military pressure (verses 3–6). The people and their leaders were placed in such distressing situations that they were compelled to either look to God in obedience or utterly forsake the Lord. They looked to God.
- **Answer:** The godly King Asa led the people into deeper national repentance and reforms. Here we learn that leadership matters (verses 8–19).

Question 4:
- **Answer:** In October of 1857, there was a stock market crash. Through this national shaking, prayer meetings proliferated throughout the nation, and hundreds of thousands of people came to saving faith in Jesus Christ.
- **Answer:** In the 1960s, John F. Kennedy, Martin Luther King Jr., and Robert F. Kennedy were assassinated; and the Vietnam War, social unrest, and racism escalated. In the midst of this chaos, broad teenage rebellion took hold, along with drugs and free sex. Yet at the same time, the Jesus Movement exploded on the scene with its many radical conversions.

Question 5:
- **Answer:** They will serve God (Isa. 2:3–4).
- **Answer:** No longer will one nation be in conflict with another nation (Isa. 2:4; Rev. 22:1–3).
Answer: Their diversity will be celebrated (Rev. 21:23–26). For nations to have glory (ESV) and splendor (NIV) to bring into the New Jerusalem, they must have diversity in their products and in their culture. Some examples of this might be the pyramids of Egypt, the philosophers of Greece, the Spanish Armada, the freedom of America, the cedar

trees of Lebanon, the oil of Saudi Arabia, the inventions of China, the cultural arts of France, etc. These have brought glory to those nations.

Question 6:
- **Answer:** America has valued religious liberty and freedom of speech. These rights afford its citizens great opportunity to share the good news of the gospel and the truth of God's Word.
- **Answer:** America is an affluent country, and many of its people use their wealth to finance local and global mission projects.
- **Answer:** Americans want others to experience what they have. Because of this, America involves itself in the affairs of countries around the world, encouraging them to adopt principles which our founding fathers derived from the Bible.
- **Answer:** American churches send missionaries around the world.
- **Answer:** America is modeling what it is to be a nation that embraces God, and what it is to be a nation that rejects God. America was founded on the teachings of the Bible, and for many years God uniquely blessed America. As America has gradually turned its back on these principles, its moral convictions, and God Himself, she has experienced a decline.

HOW DOES GOD INTERACT WITH NATIONS?
(LESSON 2)

Review:
Last time, we concluded that while the gospel has no national or ethnic borders, nations continue to play an important role in God's redemptive plan. God is using nations to prevent mankind from collectively resisting Him, to highlight mankind's need for salvation, and to draw mankind back to Himself. Since nations are part of His plan, let's turn our attention to how God interacts with nations.

Insight:
God interacts with nations by both blessing and judging the people for their actions (Deut. 11:26–28; Psa. 33:12–15; 67:4). Scripture is clear that God will protect and provide for the people of any nation where a sizeable portion of the people and the leadership walk in righteousness. Certainly, America has been one of those nations. However, Scripture is also clear that God will judge nations that choose to ignore or walk away from Him.

> **Question 1:** According to Isaiah 28:1–10 and Obadiah 1:1–4, why does God judge nations?

_____

_____

_____

_____

_____

_____

_____

Insight:
God also judges nations for specific deeds. Examples:
- Ninevah suffered because of one who plotted evil against the Lord and counseled wickedness (Nah. 1:11).
- Ninevah was judged for its cruelty to other nations beside Israel, its sexual immorality, its seduction of others, and its occult practices (Nah. 3:1, 4, 19).
- Babylon was plundered because it had plundered many nations (Hab. 2:8).
- All nations will be judged for scattering the Jews among the nations, dividing the Jewish land, casting lots for the Jewish people, trading a boy for a prostitute, and selling a girl for wine (Joel 3:2–3).
- Egypt and Edom will be judged for shedding innocent blood in the land of Judah (Joel 3:19).
- Moab's fortresses were burned because it had burned to lime the bones of Edom's king (Amos 2:1–2).

- Moab was judged for worshiping the false god Chemosh (Jer. 48:13, 35).
- Egypt was judged for worshiping idols in Memphis (Eze. 30:13).
- Judah was judged for its complacency and pursuit of comfort while refusing to grieve over its spiritual waywardness (Amos 6:1–7).

Question 2: According to Isaiah 24:1–6, why will God judge all the nations?

_____

_____

_____

_____

_____

_____

_____

Insight:
The biblical idea of judgment is broader than our American understanding of judgment. In his book *God's Judgments*, Steven Keillor presents the Hebrew idea behind the verb *shaphat* and the noun *mishpat*, which are often translated in the Old Testament as "to judge" and "the judgments."
- *Shaphat* means "to rule" or "to judge," but the Hebrews did not have our American separation of government powers, so lawmaking, law-applying, and law-enforcing powers are all included in the Hebrew concept of judging. It denotes power directed toward right ends.
- *Mishpat* has more meanings, and the context is key. Unlike the way we view judges in the American legal system today, it is not a passive impartiality that delegates action to someone else. Instead, it is a proactive right-doing that sees injustice, steps in to rescue the righteous victim, and carries out a just verdict.

The biblical idea of judgment includes a salvation aspect. Saving victims and judging wrongdoers are linked together. There is a sifting-out process in which the righteous are identified and distinguished from the wicked so that God may accomplish justice by saving the righteous. As such, God's judgment is not merely negative, being punitive or destructive. Instead, it includes a creative element in separating a righteous remnant from evildoers. For example, in the Old Testament God judged the nations to save Israel from their hostility, and He judged Israel to preserve its purity so that it could proclaim His saving power to the nations.

Anglican theologian Oliver O'Donovan has said, "Yhwh exercises his judgment by making the just and the unjust causes manifestly distinct." He goes on to explain that evil people no longer have such confusing influence over the population because the evil of their deeds is made clear to all.

Question 3: In our nation, what historical events or circumstances might have been used by God to sift-out the righteous from the unrighteous? How have these events or circumstances made the just and unjust causes within our country manifestly distinct?

_____

_____

_____

_____

_____

_____

Question 4: God's judgment includes a creative element—a redemptive purpose. According to Isaiah 26:9 and 1 Peter 4:17, what redemptive purposes might God be accomplishing by sending judgment to a nation?

_____

_____

_____

_____

_____

_____

Question 5: What additional redemptive purposes might God have for sending judgment to a nation?

_____

_____

_____

_____

_____

_____

_____

Insight:

The Bible reminds us that God's judgments are just. No nation is exempt from God's judgment if it sins. Even Israel, God's covenant people, experienced judgment.

Question 6: How does an understanding of God's judgment of nations in history influence your perspective of America's relationship to God?

_____

_____

_____

_____

_____

_____

Insight:

God wants to redeem the peoples of the earth. To accomplish this, He both blesses and judges nations according to their obedience. At the heart of both blessing and judgment are God's redemptive purposes.

Prayer Points:
-   Remembering that the leader is the representative head of the people, ask God to build righteous character within our local, state, and national leaders.
-   Ask God to graciously influence your friends, family, and coworkers so that they are ready to respond in faith when the next sifting comes to our nation.
-   Ask God to give you a greater burden for seeing people come to faith than you have for seeing our nation protected and blessed.

Insight Answers for Questions
(How Does God Interact with Nations?)

Question 1:
- **Answer:** Because of wayward national pride or a ruler's arrogance. Keep in mind that the ruler served as the representative head for the people of his kingdom.

Question 2:
- **Answer:** God will judge the nations because the inhabitants of the earth have polluted the world through immorality, have transgressed God's laws, and have broken covenant with Him (verses 5–6).

Question 3:
- **Answer:** Perhaps catastrophic events such as the Great Depression, September 11, and Hurricane Katrina. Or perhaps military conflicts such as the Civil War, World Wars I and II, the Cold War, the Iraq War, and the war in Afghanistan. If so, God may have been revealing those who would humble themselves, repent, and seek Him, versus those who would choose to further harden their hearts and continue to live contrary to God's will and ways.
- **Answer:** Perhaps social crises such as feminism, the Civil Rights Movement, Vietnam protests, AIDS, the LGBT movement, and Black Lives Matter. If so, God may have been revealing those who are willing to respect authority versus those who are rebellious at heart. Also, God may have been revealing those who appreciate that mankind is created in God's image versus those who have no respect for how God has designed and purposed mankind.
- **Answer:** Perhaps economic uncertainty, such as Black Thursday, the Dot-com Crash, the 2008 Crisis, and the $20+ trillion U.S. national debt. If so, God may have been revealing those who were honest and whose treasure rested in the Lord versus those whose hearts were self-centered, materialistic, and greedy.
- **Answer:** Perhaps judicial battles and rulings such as *Roe v. Wade* (right to have an abortion), *Obergefell v. Hodges* (right to same-sex marriage), *People v. Robert Crouse* and many other such cases (right to use marijuana), *Gonzales v. Oregon* (right for physician-assisted suicide), *Burwell v. Hobby Lobby* (right for a for-profit corporation to claim tax exemption due to religious beliefs), *Zubik v. Burwell* (right for religious organizations to claim tax exemption due to religious beliefs), and *Ingersoll v. Arlene's Flowers* (right to deny use of creative skills to celebrate something that contradicts personal religious beliefs). If so, God may have been revealing who would stand firm on the truth and relevancy of His Word regarding many cultural issues versus who would compromise by accepting worldly positions.
- **Answer:** Perhaps health concerns such as Anthrax, Bird Flu (H5N1), Swine Flu (H1N1), Severe Acute Respiratory Syndrome (SARS), Methicillin-Resistant Staphylococcus Aureus (MRSA), and Ebola. If so, God may have been revealing those whose confidence and safety rests in the Lord versus those who place their security in human efforts.
- **Answer:** Perhaps mass shootings such as in schools (University of Texas Clock Tower Shootings, Columbine High School, Virginia Tech, Red Lake High School, Sandy Hook Elementary School); in churches (Charleston, Selma, Knoxville, Maryville, Colorado Springs); in restaurants (Kileen, San Ysidro); on military bases

(Washington Navy Yard, Chattanooga); and elsewhere (the Aurora theater, the gay nightclub in Orlando, and the Beltway Sniper). Or perhaps successful and attempted terrorist acts such as the Unabomber attacks, the Shoe Bomber, the Underwear Bomber, the Black Day of Terror, the Brooklyn Bridge Plot, the NYC Subway Plot, the Boston Marathon Bombing, Fort Hood, and the Orlando Nightclub Massacre. If so, God may have been revealing those who respect human life versus those who do not value it.

Question 4:

- **Answer:** Creating a people who embrace righteousness. Times of national trouble often expose the error of our thinking and of our actions. This provokes some to seek what is right and true. People generally learn their most important lessons during seasons of adversity.
- **Answer:** God's house is purified during times of judgment, and God uses the church to model His standard of holiness for the world. When God refines His own people, His glory is revealed with greater intensity through His church.

Question 5:

- **Answer:** The saving of souls. Historically, times of national trouble provoke people to seek the Lord and His answers.
- **Answer:** Stopping the proliferation of evil. During times of national trouble, people either turn from their pursuit and propagation of evil, or they are often destroyed because of their wickedness

IS GOD ON AMERICA'S SIDE?
(LESSON 3)

Review:

As we continue our study of God's justice and its implications for nations today, keep in mind that our goal is to learn how to better stand firm now and through greater difficulties in the future, and to learn how to minister with more fruitfulness, both now and in the future. Furthermore, we want to be alerted to what the Bible teaches about nations in general—and our nation in particular. God is actively redeeming the nations, and we want to better understand how He is accomplishing this.

Last time, we learned that God's judgments are just. No nation is exempt from judgment if it sins. In this lesson we hope to answer the question, "Is God on America's side?" If God is on our side, then we can live day to day confident of our future; but if God is not on America's side, then we need to understand the seriousness of the situation and make appropriate adjustments.

Insight:

God can both bless and curse any nation (Deut. 11:26–28). After blessing a nation, God may also choose to curse a nation. Israel, who was God's covenant people, experienced both blessings and curses from God according to their obedience (Leviticus 26:1–46; Deut. 28:1–68). We tend to focus on God's blessings to the exclusion of His judgments. R. C. Sproul once challenged, "We allow for God's providence as long as it is a blessing, but we have no room for God's providence if that providence represents some kind of judgment."

Question 1: Reflecting on our nation's history, how has God blessed America?

_____

_____

_____

_____

_____

_____

Question 2: "God Bless America" is enthusiastically sung by most Americans, and after tragic events it is common to see signs which invoke the blessing of God. What do you think most Americans mean when they ask God to bless America?

_____

_____

_____

_____

_____

_____

_____

Insight:

God's warning to Israel serves as a principle for all nations: "Choose God and receive blessing, or disobey God and be cursed" (Deut. 11:26–28).

Question 3: Americans desire to be blessed by God, but do you think Americans have chosen to follow the necessary path of obedience to God in order to receive this blessing? Why or why not?

_____

_____

_____

_____

_____

_____

Question 4: What about Christians in America? Have American Christians chosen to follow the path of obedience to God necessary to receive His blessing? Why or why not?

_____

_____

_____

_____

_____

_____

Insight:

God judges nations based on the amount of spiritual light, truth, and opportunity they are given (Rom. 2:12–15). Responsibility is based on knowledge. Jesus taught that those who know God's will and don't do it will be judged more severely (Luke 12:47–48). The principle of apportioned judgment is also seen in the book of Hebrews. Because the revelation of God under the New Covenant is so much greater—that is, since Jesus came to earth and the Scriptures have been written and passed down to us—the penalty for neglecting grace is much more severe (Heb. 2:1–4).

Question 5: In what ways have Americans been granted unprecedented access to the truth of God's Word and to opportunities to growth in the Christian faith?

_____

_____

_____

_____

_____

_____

Question 6: If God became Israel's enemy, willing to fight against His own people due to their rebellion, then He can become the enemy of any nation—including our own (Isa. 63:7–10). Do you believe that we in America are in danger of having God become our enemy?

_____

_____

_____

_____

_____

_____

Insight:

No nation can claim that God is on its side. In his book *Is God on America's Side?*, Erwin Lutzer notes that God is not an American; neither is He Mexican, Russian, German, French, Chinese, or any other nationality. God does not favor one nation over another nation based on ethnic loyalties. Instead, God favors nations based on their obedience to His commands. In his book *The Divided States of America,* Richard Land writes:

> What liberal and conservatives both are missing is that America has been blessed by God in unique ways—we are not just another country, but neither are we God's special people. I do not believe that America is God's chosen nation. God established one chosen nation and people: the Jews. We are not Israel. We do not have "God on our side." We are not God's gift to the world. . . . America does not have a special claim on God. Millions of Americans do, however, believe God has a special claim on them—and their country.

Insight:

We must be on God's side. When asked whether God was on his side, Abraham Lincoln said, "I do not care whether God is on my side; the important question is whether I am on God's side, for God is always right."

When approaching Jericho, Joshua saw what most scholars believe to be the pre-incarnate Jesus Christ. In this passage, He is described as a man with a sword in his hand. Given the fact that the Israelites were actively invading the land of Canaan at this time, Joshua reasonably asked, "Are you for us, or for our adversaries?" The answer he received was, "No; but I am the commander of the army of the Lord" (Josh. 5:13–14). God wasn't choosing sides between two armies. Instead, there was God's side and everyone else's side.

If ever there was a time for God to be on Israel's side, this was it. God had personally led the Israelites to this land which He had promised to their forefathers. He had supernaturally dried up the Jordan River so that they could cross into this land, and He was about to miraculously collapse the walls of Jericho. Nevertheless, Jesus tells Joshua that He is not on Israel's side; neither is He on the side of their enemies. Instead, he commands the hosts of heaven, so Joshua had best be sure to be on His side.

Question 7: What does it mean to be on God's side?

_____

_____

_____

_____

_____

_____

Insight:

God expects us to join His side, not to invoke Him to join our side. We can choose to join God in faithful obedience to Him, or we can choose to stand in opposition to Him. A nation that acts in obedience to God's commandments is a nation that need not fear judgment. However, as we learned in the last lesson, any nation is subject to judgment if it sins. God is willing to fight against His own people at times (Isa. 63:7–10). If God became Israel's enemy, then He can become the enemy of any nation, including ours.

Prayer Points:

- Similar to when Jesus assessed the good and the bad within the seven churches in Revelation, ask God to give discernment on how He is pleased with you and how you are at odds with His purposes today (Rev 2:1–3:22).
- Ask God to have mercy on our wayward nation.
- Affirm that you are on God's side by praying a prayer of consecration.

Question 1:
- **Answer:** Americans have experienced an unprecedented level of freedom. These freedoms are secured in the U.S. Constitution, which promotes the same individual human freedoms taught in the Bible.
- **Answer:** God has protected America. Our military has been blessed to be undefeated, and there has been no sustained attack upon our homeland.
- **Answer:** America became the world's largest economy in 1871 and continued to hold this distinction until recently . . . depending on how one measures China's economy.
- **Answer:** God blessed America with two Great Awakenings and several other mighty movements of His Holy Spirit.

Question 2:
- **Answer:** In his book *Is God on America's Side?*, Erwin Lutzer answers this question, "Lord, I pray that you will protect us; especially I pray that my family might not die."
- **Answer:** In his book *Is God on America's Side?*, Erwin Lutzer answers this question, "May I live in good health; may I be able to pay the mortgage, and above all, may the stock market not fall so my retirement remains secure."
- **Answer:** By asking God to bless us we are often asking Him to affirm our lifestyles regardless of how sinful we are. Often, we want Him to give us the money and free time necessary to indulge ourselves in whatever activities we enjoy most.

Question 3:
- **Answer:** No. God is consistently banished from science, economics, history, education, and government.
- **Answer:** No. Increasingly, citizens are permitted freedom of religion provided they only exercise it in private, not in public.
- **Answer:** No. Former President Barack Obama announced that America is no longer a Christian nation. *Newsweek* magazine published an article titled "The End of Christian America." The author of this article, Jon Meacham, wrote a *New York Times* opinion piece titled "A Nation of Christians Is Not a Christian Nation," and Norman Wirzba wrote a *Washington Post* opinion piece titled "Why We Can Now Declare the End of 'Christian America.'" Also, *Newsweek* magazine published an article titled "U.S. Views on God and Life Are Turning Hindu."

Question 4:
- **Answer:** No. Despite God's command not to forsake meeting together, church attendance is in decline (Heb. 10:24–25).
  Answer: No. The national divorce rate among Christians is not lower than among those who do not claim to be Christian.
- **Answer:** No. Many mainline denominations have embraced the practices of homosexuality and transgenderism, have denied that the Bible is the infallible and inspired Word of God that is applicable for all generations, and have replaced Jesus' Great Commission with social justice causes.

- **Answer:** No. The lifestyles, attitudes, goals, and beliefs of those within the church are increasingly indistinguishable from those outside of the church.
- **Answer:** Yes. There is still a remnant of Jesus-followers who are seeking God, diligently stepping out in faith, and obeying His Word.

Question 5:

- **Answer:** Many of our nation's colleges and universities were founded with the intention of training men for Christian ministry. Although several of these institutions no longer have the Bible as their foundation, there remain many Christian colleges and universities in America today.
- **Answer:** We have ready access to Christian radio, television, books, websites, and churches.
- **Answer:** The Bible is readily available to everyone.
- **Answer:** Our freedom to access Christian content, believe what we want to believe, and speak what we believe is protected by our legal system.

Question 6:

- **Answer:** Yes.

Question 7:

- **Answer:** We fight for the same objectives and goals as God.
- **Answer:** Our motivation matches God's motivation.
- **Answer:** Our methods match God's methods.

IN WHAT WAYS IS AMERICA IN JEOPARDY? (PART 1)
(LESSON 4)

Review:

Last time, we concluded that God does not choose sides. We choose to join God's side in faithful obedience to Him, or we choose to stand in opposition to Him. Over the first three lessons, we focused on identifying biblical principles related to all nations with only brief references to our nation. In this lesson and the next, we hope to shift the focus of what the Bible teaches to the implications for America.

Question 1: According to Jeremiah 18:7–10, how does God respond to nations?

_____

_____

_____

_____

_____

_____

Insight: Jeremiah is the only prophet in the Bible who was designated by God as "a prophet to the nations" (Jer. 1:4–10). God interacts with all nations. Throughout history, God has interacted not only with Israel, but also with *all nations* ... and He still does today.

Question 2: Are you concerned about the trajectory of our nation? If yes, then in what ways has America significantly changed within your lifetime?

_____

_____

_____

_____

_____

_____

Insight:
Leviticus 18 speaks of sins for which God judges nations: incest, adultery, infanticide, bestiality, and homosexuality (Lev. 18:1–30). Because of these sins, God judged nations, casting them out of the land (Lev. **18:24–25**). Because of these sins, God eventually judged His covenant nation of Israel, as He had warned them He would do (Lev. **18:26–28**). Since God judged both Israel and other nations using these five areas as criteria for making His judgments, let's evaluate how America is doing in each of these areas.

Question 3: Does America condone and practice the sin of incest?

_____

_____

_____

_____

_____

_____

_____

Question 4: Does America condone and practice the sin of adultery?

_____

_____

_____

_____

_____

_____

Question 5: Does America condone and practice the sin of infanticide?

_____

_____

_____

_____

_____

_____

_____

Question 6: Does America condone and practice the sin of bestiality?

_____

_____

_____

_____

_____

_____

Question 7: Does America condone and practice the sin of homosexuality?

_____

_____

_____

_____

_____

Question 8: Should we be concerned if we as a nation celebrate and flaunt the very sins for which God judged other nations?

_____

_____

_____

_____

_____

_____

_____

Question 9: Why should America be exempt from judgment?

_____

_____

_____

_____

_____

_____

Prayer Points:
- Ask God for wisdom concerning how to impart biblical values to your children, grandchildren, and throughout the church, especially in the area of sexual purity.
- When we are involved in sin, James reminds us to turn our laughter into mourning (James 4:9). With this in mind, offer prayers of brokenness and repentance over our nation's many sins.
- Cry out to God for our nation in a similar way that Habakkuk did for Judah: "O LORD . . . in wrath remember mercy" (Hab. 3:2).

Insight Answers for Questions
(In What Ways is America in Jeopardy? Part 1)

Question 1:
- **Answer:** God responds to nations according to their faithfulness to Him.

Question 2:
- **Answer:** Americans command a different level of respect internationally.
  - In a continuing trend, 2018 polls and analyses show the world has lost its respect for America.[1]
  - Russian students projected a racist image on the U.S. embassy in Moscow and unfurled a banner across the street insinuating that then-President Obama is a monkey.[2]
  - In a mock attack, Russian jets buzzed a U.S. destroyer in the Baltic Sea and in the Black Sea,[3] and a Russian spy ship patrolled 30 miles off the coast of Connecticut.[4]
  - Iran seized U.S. hostages while successfully negotiating a nuclear deal.[5]
- **Answer:** Americans possess a different level of freedom.
  - 80% of third-graders walked to school alone in 1980, but by 1990, only 9% did.[6]
  - Debra Harrell was arrested for allowing her 9-year-old daughter to play in the park unattended.[7]
  - We've lost our right to privacy, with the CEOs of Facebook and Google essentially saying the age of privacy is over.[8]
  - We can't fly on an airplane without being subjected to a naked-body scanner or a full-body pat-down.
- **Answer:** Americans hold to a different moral standard.
  - As of 2018, physician-assisted suicide is legal in seven states and the District of Columbia.[9]
  - Officials in Seattle, New York, San Francisco, and Philadelphia have proposed heroin injection clinics.[10]
  - In 2015 former President Obama ordered all public schools to permit students to use bathrooms and locker rooms that match one's gender identity.[11]
  - The Supreme Court ruled on June 26, 2015, that same-sex marriages are a constitutional right.[12]
  - Business owners have been taken to court for exercising their religious moral convictions by refusing to use their talents to celebrate same-sex marriages.[13]
  - In 2016 a judge ruled Jamie Shupe to be gender non-binary,[14] and in 2018 California began offering a gender non-binary option on birth certificates.[15]
  - As of 2018, three parent families are legal in 7 states and the District of Columbia,[16] and in 2018 a woman in Florida married a tree.[17]

Question 3:
- **Answer:** No.
  - Most states prohibit sexual intercourse with any close relative.
  - Parent-child sexual relations are illegal in all fifty states.

Question 4:
- **Answer:** Yes. Americans *celebrate and flaunt* the sin of adultery.
  - Hollywood has striven to glamorize adultery with such movies as *Unfaithful*, *Election*, *American Beauty*, *Indecent Proposal*, and scores more.
  - Popular televisions shows include titles such as *Adulterers*, *The Affair*, *Californication*, *Real Wife Swap*, *Swingers*, etc. The *Los Angeles Times* reported, "Prime-time TV is starting to look like an ad for Ashley Madison, the online dating service for married folks, where the message is, 'Life is short. Have an affair.'"[18]
  - In the popular television show *Scandal*, Kerry Washington began an affair with the then-Governor Grant III. It has aired seven seasons and was named a Television Program of the Year by the American Film Institute, received the Peabody Award for Excellence in Television, and was honored as Outstanding Drama Series at the Image Awards. Also, Olivia Pope, who plays Kerry Washington, has won the Image Award for Outstanding Actress in a Drama Series and has been nominated for an Emmy Award for Outstanding Lead Actress in a Drama Series, a Golden Globe Award for Best Actress in a Drama Series, and a Screen Actor's Guild Award for Outstanding Performance by and Actress in a Drama Series.
  - Many celebrities do not limit their adultery to the movies and television but are frequently in the news for salacious affairs. Often these are not condemned but are eagerly followed and encouraged by fans.
  - The 2018 *60 Minutes* interview with porn-star Stormy Daniels about her alleged affair with President Donald Trump was its highest rated show in a decade.[19]

Question 5:
- **Answer:** Yes. Americans *celebrate and flaunt* the sin of infanticide.
  - A major party's presidential nominee advocated late-term partial birth abortion during a nationally televised debate.[20]
  - After discovering in 2015 that Planned Parenthood was selling baby parts for profit, government leaders, reporters, and activists strongly advocated on its behalf, arguing against any effort to remove taxpayer funding for the organization.
  - When Neil Gorsuch was nominated for the Supreme Court, the initial concern expressed by his opponents was a fear that he might advocate the overturning of *Roe v. Wade*.
  - As of 2018, more than 60 million babies have been aborted in America since *Roe v. Wade* in 1973.[21]

Question 6:
- **Answer:** No, but there is movement in this direction.
  - In 2011, the Senate approved a bill that legalized sodomy and bestiality in the U.S. military.[22]
  - *New York Magazine* published a 62,000 word interview favorably portraying a man who is married to a woman but who has regular sex with horses.[23]

Question 7:

- **Answer:** Yes. Americans *celebrate and flaunt* the sin of homosexuality.
    - In *Obergefell v. Hodges*, the Supreme Court determined that same-sex marriages are a constitutional right.[24]
    - Graphic homosexual relationships are openly portrayed in movies and on popular television shows, and songs like Katy Perry's "I Kissed a Girl" and Macklemore's "Same Love" top the music charts.
    - According to the Pew Research Center, Americans are becoming progressively supportive of same-sex marriages, with an 8–9% rise in approval for each successive generation.[25]
    A growing number of Christian denominations are embracing homosexuality. "In 2015, Rob Bell, former pastor of the Michigan mega-church Mars Hill said in response to a question asked by Oprah Winfrey, "The church is moments away from accepting gay marriage.""[26]

Question 8:

- **Answer:** Yes. At the very least, it should cause us to question whether our national relationship with God is as strong as we'd like to believe it to be. Perhaps we as a nation are in a precarious position before God.

Question 9:

- **Answer:** We should not be exempt from judgment. Only God's mercy has prevented America from experiencing God's judgment.

END NOTES

1. According to the 2018 Anholt-Gfk Nation Brands Index, which ranks 50 countries according to the power and quality of their brand image, the U.S. ranked 6th in 2017, a decline from its first place ranking in 2016. ("Anholt-Gfk Nation Brands Index," Gfk, n.d. Accessed April 16, 2018. http://nation-brands.gfk.com.)

    Ray, Julie. "World's Approval of U.S. Leadership Drops to New Low." *Gallup*, January 18, 2018. Accessed April 16, 2018. http://news.gallup.com/poll/225761/world-approval-leadership-drops-new-low.aspx.

    Johnson, Courtney. "Fewer People in Latin America See the U.S. Favorably Under Trump." *Pew Research Center*, April 12, 2018. Accessed April 16, 2018. http://www.pewglobal.org/2018/04/12/fewer-people-in-latin-america-see-the-u-s-favorably-under-trump/.

    "U.S. News Best Countries Ranking." *U.S. News and World Report*, n.d. Accessed April 16, 2018. https://www.usnews.com/news/best-countries/rankings-index.

2. Raymond, Adam. "Subtle Russian Light Show Depicts President Obama with a Banana in His Mouth." *New York Magazine*, August 7, 2014. Accessed April 16, 2018. http://nymag.com/daily/intelligencer/2014/08/obama-sucks-on-banana-in-russian-light-show.html.

3. Gibbon-Neff, Thomas. "A Strange Recent History of Russian Jets Buzzing Navy Ships." *The Washington Post*, April 14, 2016. Accessed April 16, 2018. https://www.washingtonpost.com/news/checkpoint/wp/2016/04/14/a-strange-recent-history-of-russian-jets-buzzing-navy-ships/?noredirect=on&utm_term=.fa4578a33d06.

4. Browne, Ryan and Barbara Starr. "Russian Spy Ship Lurks Off Connecticut Coast." CNN, n.d. Last Updated February 16, 2017. Accessed April 16, 2018. https://www.cnn.com/2017/02/15/politics/russian-spy-plane-off-connecticut-coast/.

5. Tully, Shawn. "5 Things You Need to Know About the $400 Million America Sent to Iran." *Fortune*, August 5, 2016. Accessed April 16, 2018. http://fortune.com/2016/08/05/money-america-iran/.

6. Grose, Jessica and Hanna Rosin. "The Shortening Leash." *Slate*, August 6, 2014. Accessed April 16, 2018. http://www.slate.com/articles/life/family/2014/08/slate_childhood_survey_results_kids_today_have_a_lot_less_freedom_than_their.html.

7. Wallace, Kelly. "Mom Arrested for Leaving 9-Year-Old Alone at Park." CNN, n.d. Last Updated July 21, 2014. https://www.cnn.com/2014/07/21/living/mom-arrested-left-girl-park-parents/.

8. Dvorak, John. "Eric Schmidt, Google and Privacy." *MarketWatch*, December 11, 2009. Accessed April 16, 2018. https://www.marketwatch.com/story/eric-schmidt-google-and-privacy-2009-12-11.

9. "State-by-State Guide to Physician-Assisted Suicide." ProCon.org, n.d. Last Updated April 9, 2018. Accessed April 16, 2018. https://euthanasia.procon.org/view.resource.php?resourceID=000132.

10. Ewing, Maura. "Protecting Heroin Clinics from Prosecution." *The Atlantic*, October 5, 2017. Accessed April 16, 2018. https://www.theatlantic.com/politics/archive/2017/10/philadelphia-drugs-heroin/541995/.

11. Korte, Gregory. "Schools Must Allow Transgender Bathrooms, Department of Education Says." *USA Today*, May 12, 2016. Last Updated May 13, 2016. Accessed April 16, 2018. https://www.usatoday.com/story/news/politics/2016/05/12/feds-schools-transgender-bathrooms-letter-title-ix/84311104/.

12. Fisher, Daniel. "Supreme Court Rules Same-Sex Marriage Is a Constitutional Right." *Forbes*, June 26, 2015. Accessed April 16, 2018. https://www.forbes.com/sites/danielfisher/2015/06/26/supreme-court-rules-same-sex-marriage-is-a-constitutional-right/#332fcfa5cdd0.

13. Parloff, Roger. "Christian Bakers, Gay Weddings, and a Question for the Supreme Court." *The New Yorker*, March 6, 2017. Accessed April 16, 2018. https://www.newyorker.com/news/news-desk/christian-bakers-gay-weddings-and-a-question-for-the-supreme-court.

14. Karimi, Faith and Dani Stewart. "Army Veteran Legally Not Male or Female, Judge Rules." CNN, n.d. Last Updated June 12, 2016. Accessed April 16, 2018. https://www.cnn.com/2016/06/11/us/jamie-shupe-non-binary/.

15. Caron, Christina. "Californians Will Soon have Nonbinary as a Gender Option on Birth Certificates." *The New York Times*, October 19, 2017. Accessed April 16, 2016. https://www.nytimes.com/2017/10/19/us/birth-certificate-nonbinary-gender-california.html.

16. Emanuel, Gabrielle. "Three (Parents) Can be a Crowd, but for Some It's a Faulty Family." NPR, All Things Considered, March 30, 2014. Accessed April 16, 2018. https://www.npr.org/2014/03/30/296851662/three-parents-can-be-a-crowd-but-for-some-its-a-family.

17. Miller, Andrea. "Woman Marries a 100-Year-Old Tree in Hopes of Saving it from Being Cut Down." ABC News, March 26, 2018. Accessed April 16, 2018. http://abcnews.go.com/US/woman-marries-100-year-tree-hopes-saving-cut/story?id=54014598.

18. Stanley, T.L. "Prime-Time TV Gets in Bed – and Other Places – with Adulterers." *Los Angeles Times*, December 28, 2011. Accessed April 16, 2018. http://articles.latimes.com/2011/dec/28/entertainment/la-et-adultery-20111228.

19. Rhodan, Maya. "The Stormy Daniels Interview Gave '60 Minutes' Its Highest Ratings in Years." *TIME*, March 26, 2018. Accessed April 16, 2018. http://time.com/5215421/stormy-daniels-60-minutes-ratings/.

20. Blake, Aaron. "The Final Trump-Clinton Debate Transcript, Annotated." *The Washington Post*, October 19, 2016. Accessed April 16, 2018. https://www.washingtonpost.com/news/the-fix/wp/2016/10/19/the-final-trump-clinton-debate-transcript-annotated/?nid&utm_term=.689ec18c3e78.

21. "Number of Abortions – Abortion Counters." US Abortion Clock, n.d. Accessed April 16, 2018. http://www.numberofabortions.com.

22. Queer Voices. "U.S. Military Hit with Bestiality, Sodomy Controversy after 'Don't Ask, Don't Tell Repeal." *The Huffington Post*, n.d. Last Updated February 2, 2016. https://www.huffingtonpost.com/2011/12/09/us-military-bestiality-controversy_n_1139357.html.

23. Loli, Eugenia. "What It's Like to Date a Horse." *New York Magazine*, November 20, 2014. Accessed April 16, 2018. http://nymag.com/scienceofus/2014/11/what-its-like-to-date-a-horse.html.

24. Fisher, Daniel. "Supreme Court Rules Same-Sex Marriage Is a Constitutional Right." *Forbes*, June 26, 2015. Accessed April 16, 2018. https://www.forbes.com/sites/danielfisher/2015/06/26/supreme-court-rules-same-sex-marriage-is-a-constitutional-right/#332fcfa5cdd0.

25. "Angry Silents, Disengaged Millennials: The Generation Gap and the 2012 Election." *Pew Research Center*, November 3, 2011. Accessed April 16, 2018. http://www.people-press.org/files/legacy-pdf/11-3-11%20Generations%20Release.pdf.

26. Bunte, Matt. "Rob Bell on Gay Marriage: 'We're Moments Away' from Church Embracing It." *MLive*, February 16, 2015. Accessed April 16, 2018. http://www.mlive.com/living/grand-rapids/index.ssf/2015/02/rob_bell_on_gay_marriage_were.html.

IN WHAT WAYS IS AMERICA IN JEOPARDY? (PART 2)
(LESSON 5)

Review:

Last time, we concluded that America's relationship with God might not be as strong as we'd like to believe it to be. We might be in a precarious position before God because we celebrate and flaunt the very sins for which God has judged nations in the past. During the first three lessons, we focused on identifying biblical principles related to all nations, with only brief references to our nation. In the last lesson, we began studying the implication of these biblical principles for America. In this lesson we hope to continue studying the implications for America.

Question 1: What are the two types of judgment recorded in Amos 4:1–12?

_____

_____

_____

_____

_____

_____

_____

Teaching Insight:

A corrective judgment can be severe because it may require something extreme to capture the attention of the people. Despite the severity of God's judgment against the Israelites, they failed to realize that they were a nation under judgment. Perhaps this is because God often uses natural means to accomplish His purposes. As such, the Israelites may have dismissed God's warning signals of famine, drought, disease, etc. as natural events.

Could it be that, like Israel, we are dismissing as natural events God's efforts to arouse us from our spiritual slumber? Like Israel, America is experiencing trouble in the areas of:
- **Water** –In 2017 Texas and Florida were inundated with flood waters from record-breaking hurricanes,[1,2] while 10 western states suffered from 62 active forest fires, due in part to a lack of water.[3] In February of 2018, 38.4% of the nation experienced drought conditions.[4]
- **Lack of Food** – As of 2018, 41 million Americans struggle with hunger,[5] and one in six American children may not know where they will get their next meal.[6]
- **Poor Harvests** - In 2017 America experienced 16 separate billion-dollar weather and climate-related disasters, costing American agriculture more than $5 billion dollars in lost crops.[7]
- **Infestation** – The Emerald Ash Borer is spreading at an uncontrollable rate, killing millions of Ash trees across the country and increasing the risk of forest fires where

such are usually rare. This invasive insect has been heralded by researchers as the most serious threat to forests ever seen in the U.S.[8]

- **Disease** – Untreatable sexually transmitted diseases[9] and antibiotic-resistant bacteria are spreading across America.[10] Our water infrastructure is stressed, producing an increase in waterborne diseases.[11] And as of 2018, one out of every three Americans are likely to develop cancer within their lifetime.[12]

- **Foreign Attacks / Casualties of War** – Between 2014 and 2017, there have been at least 18 terrorist attacks against America linked to ISIS.[13] Countries such as China, Russia, and North Korea conduct regular cyber-attacks against Americans.[14] And as of 2017, approximately 7,000 American sons and daughters have been lost in our war against terrorism.[15]

Question 2: Do you think God might be bringing corrective judgment on America now by removing His hand of blessing and protection? If so, how?

_____

_____

_____

_____

_____

_____

_____

Question 3: How is God removing His hand of blessing in the area of economics?

_____

_____

_____

_____

_____

_____

_____

Insight for the Above Question:
God judges nations by increasing their national debt (Deut. 28:12–13, 15, and 43–44). God also judges nations by allowing the foreigners among them to rise in stature (verse 43). U.S. businesses and infrastructure, such as toll roads and bridges, are increasingly being bought by foreigners. Furthermore, America is transforming its traditions and values to cater to the traditions and values of people from other countries.

Question 4: How is God removing His hand of blessing in the area of government?

_____

_____

_____

_____

_____

_____

Insight for the Above Question:
God judges nations by depriving their leaders of reason (Job 12:23–24).

Question 5: How is God removing His hand of blessing in the area of family?

_____

_____

_____

_____

_____

_____

Insight for the Above Question:
God judges nations by allowing the people's passions and lusts to rule them (Rom. 1:18, 26–28).

Insight:

Christian author and apologist Ravi Zacharias has said, "When God is absent, chaos is the norm." In the areas of economy, government, and the family, America fails the spiritual litmus test.

Question 6: What is preventing God from exacting a more severe form of judgment on America?

_____

_____

_____

_____

_____

_____

_____

Prayer Points:
- Ask God to give us greater insight into the spiritual implications of what we listen to on talk radio and news outlets.
- Ask God to open the eyes of our political leaders to understand what is taking place in the economy, government, and family and what is at stake.
- Cry out to God for mercy for our nation in a similar way that Daniel did (Dan. 9:1–19).

Question 1:
- **Answer:** God's judgment often comes in two phases. The first phase is a corrective judgment in which God lifts His hand of blessing and protection. John MacArthur has referred to this as the wrath of abandonment. It is designed to alert a nation to its need to repent.
  - ○ God judged His people by selectively sending rain to some cities and not to others, by a lack of food and water, poor harvests, blight and mildew, locusts, pestilence, and military attacks; yet the people refused to repent and return to God (verses 6–10).
- **Answer:** The second phase is a more severe judgment. This often involves something which shakes a nation on a fundamental level. It is designed to shake a nation hard enough to compel the people to let go of the idols to which they are clinging. This usually results in the nation either letting go of these idols or being destroyed by God.
  - ○ God judged His people by casting them out of their land, some of them even being taken away by fishhooks (verses 2–3). Also, the phrase "prepare to meet your God" carries more weight and greater consequences than when God confronted the people with various plagues (verse 12).

Question 2:
- **Answer:** Yes. Examples: As of 2018, physician-assisted suicide is legal in seven states and the District of Columbia;[16] heroine deaths increased more than 500% between 2000 and 2016;[17] mass shootings; financial crisis of 2008; racial conflict; at least 18 terrorist attacks against America linked to ISIS between 2014 and 2017;[18] New York City officially recognizing 31 genders;[19] etc.
- **Answer:** Yes. There are cracks in our economic foundation, our government, and the family unit.

Question 3:
- **Answer:** The U.S. dollar has been devalued.
  - ○ A $1.00 item in 1990 cost $1.91 in 2018.[20]
  - ○ Since the creation of the Federal Reserve in 1913, the U.S. dollar has lost over 96% of its purchasing power. This means that today's dollar would be worth less than four cents in 1913.[21]
- **Answer:** As of 2018, the U.S. trade deficit is over $820 billion.[22]
- **Answer:** The average debt for Americans 35–54 is nearly $135,000.[23]
  - ○ The average for Americans under 35 is $67,000.
  - ○ The average for Americans 75 and up is $34,500.
- **Answer:** The U.S. national debt reached $21 trillion in 2018.[24]
  - ○ As of 2018, U.S. debt is rising 36% faster than the economy.[25]
  - ○ U.S. debt owned by foreigners has increased from 4% in 1970 to 12% in 1985, and 34% in 2015.[26]

Question 4:

- **Answer:** There is excessive gridlock within the American government. In 2014 the House of Representatives reported that 352 bills were sitting on Senate Majority Leader Harry Reid's desk awaiting action.[27]
  - 98% of them passed the House with bipartisan support.
  - 50% of them passed the House unanimously.
  - 55 of them were introduced by Democrats.
- **Answer:** There is excessive corruption within the American government. The 2016 Democratic presidential nominee was under two federal investigations while campaigning. One of these investigations revolved around pay-for-play allegations.[28]
- **Answer:** Accusations of illegal activity and corruption have been leveled against former FBI directors Robert Mueller and James Comey, former Attorney Generals Eric Holder and Loretta Lynch, and Deputy Attorney General Rod Rosenstein.
- **Answer:** There is excessive wastefulness within the American government. The HealthCare.gov website cost more than $2 billion to create,[29] San Diego was granted $1.04 billion to expand its trolley by 10.9 miles, and $30,000 was spent on a production of "Doggie Hamelet" which involved actors shouting lines from Shakespeare while chasing dogs in an open New Hampshire field.[30]

Question 5:

- **Answer:** 40% of new marriages are likely to end in divorce.[31]
- **Answer:** In a large 2013 government survey, 50% of people cohabitated with someone before marriage, and 20% of women gave birth while cohabitating.[32]
- **Answer:** The family unit is being redefined. In *Obergefell v. Hodges*, the Supreme Court ruled that same-sex marriages are a constitutional right.[33] As of 2018, three parent families are legal in 7 states and the District of Columbia.[34] And in 2018 a woman in Florida married a tree.[35]

Question 6:

- **Answer:** Nothing except His mercy.
- **Answer:** The Bible teaches that God is great in mercy and patience, waiting for repentance, but in the face of continuous rebellion, His mercy will run out. For example, severe judgment came to Judah (the southern kingdom of Israel) in 586 B.C. (2 Kings 25:1–21; 2 Chr. 36:1–21; Jer. 39:1–10).
- **Answer:** In Genesis, God prophesied judgment against the Amorites, speaking of a time when their sins would have reached its full measure (Gen. 15:16). We do not know how God measures a nation's sins, but we do know that God has set limitations as to how far a nation may be permitted to transgress in its rebellion against Him.

END NOTES

1. Samenow, Jason. "Harvey is a 1,000-Year Flood Event Unprecedented in Scale." *The Washington Post*, August 31, 2017. Accessed April 16, 2018. https://www.washingtonpost.com/news/capital-weather-gang/wp/2017/08/31/harvey-is-a-1000-year-flood-event-unprecedented-in-scale/?utm_term=.fbc16ecc49da.

2. Regan, Adam. "Hurricane Irma Could Create One of the Largest Mass Evacuations in U.S. History." *USA Today*, April 16, 2018. Accessed September 8, 2017. https://www.usatoday.com/story/news/nation-now/2017/09/07/hurricane-irma-evacuations-florida/643045001/.

3. "National Preparedness Level 5 Report." National Interagency Fire Center, n.d. Last Updated September 13, 2017. Accessed September 13, 2017. https://www.nifc.gov/fireInfo/nfn.htm.

4. Rice, Doyle. "U.S. Drought at Worst Level in Nearly 4 Years." *USA Today*, February 2, 2018. Last Updated February 3, 2018. Accessed April 16, 2018. https://www.usatoday.com/story/weather/2018/02/02/u-s-drought-worst-level-nearly-4-years/300850002/.

5. "Hunger and Poverty Facts." Feeding America, n.d. Accessed April 16, 2018. http://www.feedingamerica.org/hunger-in-america/hunger-and-poverty-facts.html.

6. "Child Hunger Facts." Feeding America, n.d. Accessed April 16, 2018. http://www.feedingamerica.org/hunger-in-america/hunger-and-poverty-facts.html.

7. Bloch, Sam. "2017's Natural Disasters Cost American Agriculture Over $5 Billion." *The New Food Economy*, January 4, 2018. Accessed April 16, 2018. https://newfoodeconomy.org/2017-natural-disasters-agriculture-damage-5-billion/.

8. Biba, Erin. "America's Ash Trees are Being Wiped Out—Here's How You Can Help Them." *Earther*, October 17, 2017. Accessed April 18, 2018. https://earther.com/americas-ash-trees-are-being-wiped-out-heres-how-you-ca-1819618010.

9. Sarmiento, Samuel. "3 Common STDs Becoming Untreatable: How Worried Should We Be?" NBC News, September 2, 2016. Accessed April 16, 2018. https://www.nbcnews.com/health/sexual-health/3-common-stds-becoming-untreatable-what-happens-now-n642161.

10. Szabo, Liz. "'Nightmare' Bacteria, Resistant to Almost Every Drug, Stalk U.S. Hospitals." *USA Today*, April 3, 2018. Last Updated April 3, 2018. Accessed April 16, 2018. https://www.usatoday.com/story/news/nation/2018/04/03/nightmare-bacteria-antibiotic-resistant-stalk-hospitals/482162002/.

11. Rose, Joan. "America's Water Crisis Could be Worse than You Know." *TIME*, March 22, 2016. Accessed April 16, 2018. http://time.com/4266919/americas-water-crisis/.

12. "Lifetime Risk of Developing or Dying from Cancer." American Cancer Society, n.d. Last Updated January 4, 2018. Accessed April 16, 2018. https://www.cancer.org/cancer/cancer-basics/lifetime-probability-of-developing-or-dying-from-cancer.html.

13. Haltiwanger, John. "ISIS in America: How Many Times has the Islamic State Attacked the U.S.?" *Newsweek*, December 11, 2017. Accessed April 16, 2018. http://www.newsweek.com/islamic-state-america-attacks-744497.

14. Sanger, David and William Broad. "Pentagon Suggests Countering Devastating Cyberattacks with Nuclear Arms." *The New York Times*, January 16, 2018. Accessed April 16, 2018. https://www.nytimes.com/2018/01/16/us/politics/pentagon-nuclear-review-cyberattack-trump.html.

15. Lee, Kurtis. "Memorial Day: The Number of Americans Who Have Died in Battle since the Revolutionary War." *Los Angeles Times*, May 29, 2017. Accessed April 16, 2018. http://www.latimes.com/nation/la-na-memorial-day-20170529-htmlstory.html.

16. "State-by-State Guide to Physician-Assisted Suicide." ProCon.org, n.d. Last Updated April 9, 2018. Accessed April 16, 2018. https://euthanasia.procon.org/view.resource.php?resourceID=000132.

17. "The Opioid Crisis IS a Heroin Crisis in Washington State." The Evergreen at Northpoint, March 8, 2018. Accessed April 16, 2018. https://www.evergreendrugrehab.com/blog/opioid-crisis-heroin-crisis-washington-state/.

18. Haltiwanger, John. "ISIS in America: How Many Times has the Islamic State Attacked the U.S.?" *Newsweek*, December 11, 2017. Accessed April 16, 2018. http://www.newsweek.com/islamic-state-america-attacks-744497.

19. Hasson, Peter. "New York City Lets You Choose from 31 Different Gender Identities." *The Daily Caller*, May 24, 2016. Accessed April 16, 2018. http://dailycaller.com/2016/05/24/new-york-city-lets-you-choose-from-31-different-gender-identities/.

20. "Inflation Calculator." U.S. Inflation Calculator, n.d. Accessed April 16, 2018. http://www.usinflationcalculator.com.

21. Swann, Ben. "Congressman Proposes Bill to Return to Pre-1913 Gold-Backed US Dollar." The Daily Coin Blog, April 10, 2018. Accessed April 16, 2018. https://thedailycoin.org/2018/04/10/congressman-proposes-bill-to-return-to-pre-1913-gold-backed-us-dollar/.

22. "U.S. National Debt Clock." U.S. Debt Clock, n.d. Accessed April 16, 2018. http://www.usdebtclock.org.

23. Renzulli, Kerri Anne. "This is How Much Debt the Average American has Now—at Every Age." *TIME*, April 13, 2018. Accessed June 7, 2018. http://time.com/money/5233033/average-debt-every-age/.

24. "U.S. National Debt Clock." U.S. Debt Clock, n.d. Accessed April 16, 2018. http://www.usdebtclock.org.

25. Black, Simon. "The US' National Debt is Rising 36% Faster than the Economy." *Business Insider*, March 21, 2018. Accessed April 16, 2018. http://www.businessinsider.com/the-national-debt-is-rising-much-faster-than-the-economy-2018-3.

26. "Federal Debt Held by Foreign and International Investors." FRED, n.d. Accessed April 16, 2018. https://fred.stlouisfed.org/series/FDHBFIN.

27. Jacobson, Louis. "Rep. Lynn Jenkins Blames Harry Reid for 'Do-Nothing Senate.'" *Politifact*, August 6, 2014. Accessed April 26, 2018. http://www.politifact.com/truth-o-meter/statements/2014/aug/06/lynn-jenkins/rep-lynn-jenkins-blames-harry-reid-do-nothing-sena/.

28. Lucas, Fred. "'Not Over': 4 Legal Probes Hillary Clinton Still Faces." *The Daily Signal*, November 10, 2016. Accessed April 16, 2018. https://www.dailysignal.com/2016/11/10/not-over-4-legal-probes-hillary-clinton-still-faces/.

29. Wayne, Alex. "Obamacare Website Costs Exceed $2 Billion, Study Finds." *Bloomberg*, September 24, 2014. Accessed April 26, 2018. https://www.bloomberg.com/news/articles/2014-09-24/obamacare-website-costs-exceed-2-billion-study-finds.

30. Perticone, Joe. "The Most Ridiculous Projects the Government Funded in 2017." *Business Insider*, November 28, 2017. Accessed April 26, 2018. http://www.businessinsider.com/james-lankford-federal-fumbles-report-of-government-waste-2017-11.

31. "U.S. Divorce Rates and Statistics." Divorce Source, n.d. Accessed April 16, 2018. http://www.divorcesource.com/ds/main/u-s-divorce-rates-and-statistics-1037.shtml.

32. Stein, Rob. "Study: Record Number of People are Cohabitating." NPR, Morning Edition, April 4, 2013. Accessed April 16, 2018. https://www.npr.org/2013/04/04/176203263/study-record-number-of-people-are-cohabitating.

33. Green, Emma. "Gay Marriage is Now a Constitutional Right in the United States of America." *The Atlantic*, June 26, 2015. Accessed April 16, 2018. https://www.theatlantic.com/politics/archive/2015/06/gay-marriage-legal-in-the-united-states-of-america/396947/.

34. Emanuel, Gabrielle. "Three (Parents) Can be a Crowd, but for Some It's a Faulty Family." NPR, All Things Considered, March 30, 2014. Accessed April 16, 2018. https://www.npr.org/2014/03/30/296851662/three-parents-can-be-a-crowd-but-for-some-its-a-family.

35. Miller, Andrea. "Woman Marries a 100-Year-Old Tree in Hopes of Saving it from Being Cut Down." ABC News, March 26, 2018. Accessed April 16, 2018. http://abcnews.go.com/US/woman-marries-100-year-tree-hopes-saving-cut/story?id=54014598.

IN CHALLENGING DAYS, ARE CHRISTIANS PROTECTED?
(LESSON 6)

Review:

Last time, we concluded that America is likely experiencing a corrective form of judgment, and it is only God's mercy that is preventing a more severe form of judgment. Reflecting on the likelihood of some kind of national shaking ahead of us, we now need to look at our situation more personally. What does a national judgment mean for God's people? In this lesson, we hope to explore some possible answers to this question.

Insight:

The Bible teaches that sometimes God extends mercy to a nation on behalf of His righteous people living within that nation. Abraham pleaded on behalf of the city of Sodom, and God responded to his plea. God agreed to Abraham's request that He spare the city if 50 righteous individuals could be found there (Gen. 18:22–33). He then expanded His mercy as Abraham continued to intercede on behalf of the city of Sodom. God eventually told Abraham that He would spare the entire city if only 10 righteous individuals could be found. This is because God responds in mercy to the presence of the righteous and to the intercession of the righteous.

Question 1: Why do you think God was willing to spare an entire city to protect only 10 righteous people?

_____

_____

_____

_____

_____

_____

Question 2: What are some other examples in Scripture where God responded to the intercession of the righteous?

_____

_____

_____

_____

_____

_____

_____

Insight:
God's desire is not to destroy people. God's desire is that we obey Him.

Question 3: According to Jeremiah 18:7–10, what is necessary for God to relent of the judgment He has planned for a nation?

_____

_____

_____

_____

_____

_____

_____

Question 4: According to Jeremiah 18:7–10, why do you think it is important that God relent of the good He had planned for a nation if it does evil and rebels against His commands?

_____

_____

_____

_____

_____

_____

Question 5: According to 1 Peter 4:17, are God's people exempt from judgment?

_____

_____

_____

_____

_____

_____

Question 6: According to Hebrews 12:5–11, why does God judge His church if they have been forgiven of their sins?

_____

_____

_____

_____

_____

_____

Question 7: Is the American church experiencing judgment? Why might God be removing His hand of blessing in the area of the church?

_____

_____

_____

_____

_____

_____

Question 8: Are the righteous protected from the effects of God's judgment on the wicked?

_____

_____

_____

_____

_____

_____

Question 9: Are there any national sins in which the American church is participating from which we must separate?

_____

_____

_____

_____

_____

_____

_____

Question 10: Do you need to separate yourself from anything taking place in our nation or within cultural Christianity?

_____

_____

_____

_____

_____

_____

Prayer Points:

- Pray that your local church will be faithful and full of faith in the midst of challenging days.
- Ask God to make you and your Christian friends willing to stand firm in the face of insults, suffering, and even persecution.
- Ask God to fill your church with people who will see challenging days as an opportunity to grow in holiness.
- Thank God for His willingness and power to protect His children.

Question 1:
- **Answer:** When people live righteous lives, they shine like lights in the darkness (Matt. 5:14–16; Eph. 5:8–9). That light reveals the error of people's ways and the truth of God's Word. As such, righteous people allow the Holy Spirit to convict people of their sinful behavior and provide them opportunity to repent of their ways. As long as there is a remnant of righteous individuals, there remains hope that people will be drawn to Jesus Christ.
- **Answer:** God does not need a multitude to accomplish great things. He only needs a faithful few. From Abraham, God created an entire nation (Gen. 22:15–18), and using twelve apostles, God laid the foundation for the church (Eph. 2:19–21).

Question 2:
- **Answer:** When the Israelites built a golden calf to worship, God told Moses that He would destroy the people and build a new nation out of Moses. However, Moses interceded for the Israelites, and God relented (Exo. 32:7–14).
- **Answer:** God threatened to make Israel a place of ruins, but King Hezekiah interceded on behalf of the nation, and God relented (Jer. 26:18–19).
- **Answer:** When King David sinned by taking a census of Israel and Judah, God sent a plague on the people, but David interceded on behalf of the people and asked that the punishment fall instead on himself and his family. As a result, God relented (2 Sam. 24:15–17).

Question 3:
- **Answer:** Repentance. Repentance is not simply feeling bad about what we have done or asking for forgiveness. Repentance means to turn away from our evil actions and turn back to God in humble obedience.

Question 4:
- **Answer:** Without the incentive of pain and discomfort, we as humans rarely feel the need to change our behavior. God knows that being in a right relationship with Himself is more important than temporary comfort and pleasures.
- **Answer:** If God were to bless a nation that is in rebellion to Himself, it might encourage other nations to follow their example.
- **Answer:** If God continues to bless a nation that is in rebellion to Him, then could be understood by other nations to be a tacit endorsement of sinful behavior, or it may give the impression that God does not care how obedient a nation is to His commands.

Question 5:
- **Answer:** No. Before God judges nations, He will judge His church.

Question 6:

- **Answer:** Christians are God's adopted children, and Hebrews teaches that a loving father must discipline his children.
- **Answer:** While we may have been forgiven of our sins and declared to be holy by God, we do not yet live in holiness. Instead, we are in the daily process of becoming increasingly like Jesus (Rom. 8:29; 2 Cor. 3:18).
- **Answer:** God loves us too much to allow us to continue in our sin because He understands how destructive it is.
- **Answer:** If God ignores the sins of His people, then others might conclude that sinful behavior is not serious because God's people sin with impunity.

Question 7:

- **Answer:** Many Christians don't know basic doctrine.
  - 48% of Evangelicals believe God accepts the worship of all religions.[1]
  - 35% of white Evangelicals, 68% of Protestants and Catholics, and 85% of non-denominational Christians favor same-sex marriage.[2]
  - 38% of Evangelicals, 65% of Protestants, and 66% of Catholics believe mankind evolved from primitive life forms.[3]
- **Answer:** Many pastors refuse to teach biblical truth about today's key issues.
  - A Barna Group study concluded that 90% of pastors believe the Bible speaks into today's key issues, but only 10% of pastors are teaching what the Bible says about these issues.[4] We are moving toward experiencing a famine of God's Word (Amos 8:11).
- **Answer:** Many children are leaving the faith.[5]
  - 88% of children in Evangelical homes leave church at the age of 18.
  - 61% of today's young adults had been churched during their teen years but are now spiritually disengaged.
  - 63% of teenaged "Christians" don't believe that Jesus is the Son of the one true God.
  - 51% of teenaged "Christians" don't believe that Jesus rose from the dead.
  - 68% of teenaged "Christians" don't believe that the Holy Spirit is a real person.

Question 8:

- **Answer:** Sometimes. When God judged the Egyptians with swarms of flies, the Jews living in the land of Goshen were spared because they were the people of God (Ex. 8:20–23).
  Answer: Not always. When God permitted the Babylonians to conquer Judah as a judgment against their disobedience, the Babylonians took many captives. Daniel and his godly friends were among those captives. When God made the nation refugees because of their prolonged wickedness, the faithful were also uprooted and called on to survive in a pagan culture.
- **Answer:** No. If we are participating in the sins for which God is judging the nation, then we will likely experience the same consequences (Rev. 18:4). God commands His people to separate themselves from the sinful practices of the nations where they dwell. At times, God even commands His people to recognize the warning signs and to leave the nation that is clearly set apart for divine judgment.

Question 9:

-   **Answer:** Yes. Examples: Homosexuality, transgenderism, divorce, greed, self-centeredness, complacency, gossip and back-biting (perhaps through social media), etc.

END NOTES

1. "2016 State of American Theology Study." *Lifeway Research*, n.d. Accessed April 16, 2018. https://thestateoftheology.com/assets/downloads/2016-state-of-america-white-paper.pdf.

2. "Changing Attitudes on Gay Marriage." Pew Research Center, June 26, 2017. Accessed April 16, 2018. http://www.pewforum.org/fact-sheet/changing-attitudes-on-gay-marriage/.

3. Masci, David. "For Darwin Day, 6 Facts about the Evolution Debate." Pew Research Center, February 10, 2017. Accessed April 16, 2018. http://www.pewresearch.org/fact-tank/2017/02/10/darwin-day/.

4. Baldwin, Chuck. "New Research: Pastors Deliberately Keeping Flock in the Dark." Chuck Baldwin Live, August 7, 2014. Accessed April 16, 2018. https://chuckbaldwinlive.com/Articles/tabid/109/ID/1213/New-Research-Pastors-Deliberately-Keeping-Flock-In-The-Dark.aspx.

5. "The Problem." Faith Ascent Ministries, n.d. Accessed April 16, 2018. https://faithascentministries.com/the-problem/.

WILL YOU CONTRAST THE WORLD?
(LESSON 7)

Review:

Last time, we concluded that the church will not be exempt from judgment for national sins if the church is participating in those sins. Christians are called to separate themselves from worldly practices, ambitions, and attitudes (2 Cor. 6:14–7:1; Tit. 2:11–14; 1 John 2:15–17). While we are to live in the world, we are not to be *of* the world; we are called aliens in this world whose citizenship is in heaven (Php. 3:20).

We also concluded that even though God may protect His faithful followers through judgment, they are not always protected from experiencing the effects of that judgment. For example, Noah was protected, but he still had to build an ark, travel through stormy seas, and start his life over. Likewise, the lives of faithful Jewish believers were spared when Babylon attacked their nation, but they still experienced exile along with unfaithful Jews during the Babylonian exile.

Insight:

We are not called to simply keep our heads low and protect ourselves. Instead, we are to serve as beacons of light and as Christ's ambassadors to our nation (Matt. 5:14–16; 2 Cor. 5:20). Christian leaders have said that the church serves as the conscience of the nation.

Question 1: It has been said that the church serves as the conscience of the nation. Do you think this is an accurate description of today's church? How effective is the church today as a national conscience?

_____

_____

_____

_____

_____

_____

Insight:

If we wish to influence the culture of our nation, we must first live lives that contrast the culture (1 Pet. 3:14–16). The apostle Peter took for granted that any Christians who were faithfully living what they believed would stand out among their friends and coworkers.

Question 2: Can we effectively call people to a different lifestyle and a different hope when we are seen as living for the same things that spiritually lost people are living for, and when we are hoping for the same things they hope for?

_____

_____

_____

_____

_____

_____

_____

Question 3: What are some ways Christians are living for and hoping for the same things as the world?

_____

_____

_____

_____

_____

_____

_____

Question 4: Does this mean we should not listen to music, enjoy sports, drive nice vehicles, or use Facebook?

_____

_____

_____

_____

_____

_____

_____

Question 5: How much of your time is devoted to pursuing success according to the world's standards versus pursuing a greater understanding and faithfulness to God's commands?

Insight:

We should ask the question, "Am I willing to give up having a 'normal' American life in order to fulfill my calling as a Christian and to influence those around me?" The apostle Peter was under no delusion that people would respect and honor Christians for standing apart. Rather, Peter expected that men would slander, accuse, and persecute Christians for being different from them and the rest of society.

If we wish to influence our nation for Christ, then we must be willing to stand firm against the culture. It has been said, "In a time of universal deceit, telling the truth is a revolutionary act." Jesus is the greatest example of this. As disciples of Jesus Christ, we should not expect to be treated better than our Master (John 15:18–21).

Question 6: How did people respond to Jesus when He spoke the truth in love?

_____

_____

_____

_____

_____

_____

Insight:

When we speak the truth, we draw a line in the sand and compel people to choose sides. Some may receive the truth and be grateful, but others will reject it and despise us for compelling them to choose and for shedding light on their lie (John 7:4; 2 Cor. 2:14–16).

Question 7: What cultural issues may God be calling you to confront and speak truth into among your family, friends, neighbors, and coworkers?

_____

_____

_____

_____

_____

_____

_____

Prayer Points:
- Understanding that the church is to be the conscience of the nation, pray that individual Christians will be the conscience of those within their circle of influence. In other words, pray that you and your fellow Christians will boldly stand for what is right and speak the truth in love.
- Pray that you and the Christians you know will stand firm on God's Word and clearly contrast the worldly values of our culture.
- Pray that you will so love God and wholeheartedly follow Jesus that people around you will become curious to know why you are so devoted to God.

Insight Answers for Questions
(Will You Contrast the World?)

Question 1:
- **Answer:** Ineffective: The church often refuses to speak into political issues for fear of losing its tax exemption, fear of controversy, or fear of being charged with not focusing on the most important issues of the Christian faith.
- **Answer:** Ineffective: Entire denominations have embraced the practices of divorce, pre-marital sex and co-habitation, abortion, homosexuality, transgenderism, etc.
- **Answer:** Ineffective: The church has created a list of "acceptable" sins such as gossip, lying, self-centeredness, greed, hypocrisy, etc.

  Answer: Ineffective: The church often turns a blind eye to those struggling with addictions, mental illness, broken families, poverty, etc. Churches may be eager to support ministries devoted to these issues or to help causes far away, but there is often a reluctance to acknowledge and address these problems directly and on a local level.
- **Answer:** Ineffective: Many within the church enjoy the same vulgar entertainment as the world, speak like the world, dress like the world, think like the world, and share the same goals and ambitions as the world.
- **Answer:** Many within the church have rejected the Bible as the ultimate, eternal, and infallible standard for truth and practice. Science and public consensus have replaced the Bible as the true standard in our nation for determining truth and practice.
- **Answer:** Ineffective: By repeatedly choosing the wrong battles to fight, the church has acquired a reputation for being irrelevant, unloving, legalistic, and hypocritical.
- **Answer:** Somewhat effective. The church has endeavored to preserve biblical and traditional understandings of marriage, gender, the family unit, the sanctity of human life, etc. Some believers have stood boldly for truth and righteousness in the face of great immorality.

Question 2:
- **Answer:** No. How can we say that what we believe is better than what they believe if there is no practical difference in application?

Question 3:
- **Answer:** We often live for the success of our sports teams; our children's education; our careers; a comfortable retirement; bigger and nicer cars, houses, or furniture; pleasure; etc.
- **Answer:** We place our hope and confidence in the stock market and our 401K plans, the right politicians, our possessions, our jobs and income, family and relationships, etc.

Question 4:
- **Answer:** No, but if any of these activities are making us more worldly in our thinking, less godly in our actions, and more distant from the power and presence of Jesus Christ, then we need to reevaluate how we engage in these activities. We need to confess that we have departed from Jesus as our first love, repent, and do what God is calling us to do.

- **Answer:** No. Rather, it means we cannot measure our success by the same standards the world uses. Our success is not dependent on our salary, the clothes we wear, the size of our house, what school our children attend, how many followers we have on Facebook, the success of our sports team, our 401K plan, etc. Our success is measured by our faithfulness to God's commands.

Question 6:

- **Answer:** Some accepted what He said, but many mocked, hated, slandered, persecuted Him, and put Him to death.

WILL YOU TAKE NEW GROUND?
(LESSON 8)

Review:

Last time, we concluded that if we wish to influence our nation, we must be willing to contrast the culture. When we speak the truth, we draw a line in the sand and compel people to choose sides. Some may receive the truth and be grateful, but others will reject it and despise us for compelling them to choose and for shedding light on their lie (John 7:4; 2 Cor. 2:14–16). Regardless, we stand on the truth, and if we wish to influence our nation for Christ, then we must be careful not to be deceived into embracing spiritual lies ourselves.

Question 1: What does the apostle Paul mean when he says in Ephesians 4:26–27 to give no opportunity to the devil?

_____

_____

_____

_____

_____

_____

Question 2: It is interesting that the context of Ephesians 4:26–27 speaks of becoming angry. Of everything that could provide the devil a foothold, why do you think Paul chose to focus on anger?

_____

_____

_____

_____

_____

_____

Insight for the Above Question:
What begins as a campsite can become an established dwelling place, like a home.
If we are not careful, this can eventually become a stronghold. According to
2 Corinthians 10:3–5, it is when we believe spiritual lies and false arguments that a demonic
stronghold is established in our lives.

Question 3: What are lies that some in our culture have accepted which have given rise to demonic strongholds in their lives?

_____

_____

_____

_____

_____

_____

Insight:
If we wish to influence our nation, then we must engage ideas. These ideas may manifest themselves in the form of political causes, lifestyle choices, attitudes, addictions, self-mutilation, etc., but at their core is a spiritual lie. For us to engage cultural ideas and the spiritual lies which undergird them, we must be informed, as it is difficult both to identify and to engage spiritual lies when we are uninformed.

Question 4: On a scale of one to 10, how much of your knowledge is derived from the local newspaper, cable news, YouTube, Facebook, talk radio, etc., and how much is derived from the Bible and your local church?

_____

_____

_____

_____

_____

_____

Question 5: Should the local church speak into cultural issues? If so, how?

_____

_____

_____

_____

_____

_____

Question 6: What are some useful resources you can use to help educate yourself on cultural issues from a biblical perspective?

_____

_____

_____

_____

_____

_____

_____

Insight:
For us to engage cultural ideas and the spiritual lies which undergird them, we must be vocal. It matters little how informed we are if we do nothing with that information.

Question 7: When speaking into cultural issues, what should be your primary goal?

_____

_____

_____

_____

Question 8: Is there a platform available to you to communicate truth that you haven't yet taken full advantage of?

_____

_____

_____

_____

_____

_____

Question 9: Should you be afraid of offending people with the truth?

_____

_____

_____

_____

_____

_____

_____

Insight:

As Christians, we are called to challenge ideas. Having informed ourselves of the issues and familiarized ourselves with what the Bible teaches, we must be willing to take new ground by identifying and confronting the ideological lies of the enemy.

Question 10: What are some specific topics you would like to further research so that you can effectively speak into the culture?

_____

_____

_____

_____

_____

_____

_____

Prayer Points:
- Ask God to show you individually, and your church body corporately, what lies you have believed that could develop into strongholds.
- Ask God what cultural issues you need to study to be informed enough to influence the culture.
- Ask God what cultural issues your church needs to address to make Christians more influential.
- Ask God how He might want you to use social media to speak into the issues of our culture.

Question 1:
- **Answer:** The Greek word translated as "opportunity" (ESV), "foothold" (NIV), or "place" (KJV) is *topos*, and it can mean a lot of things. Generally, it carries the idea of a place and can also be translated as a spot, a space, a room, a location, or a dwelling place.
- **Answer:** The apostle Paul commands us not to give the devil any opportunity to set up camp in our hearts.

Question 2:
- **Answer:** We tend not to think as clearly when we are angry, which makes us more susceptible to believing lies and false arguments.

Question 3:
- **Answer:** God just wants us to be happy.
- **Answer:** God doesn't care who we love, simply that we love (homosexuality).
- **Answer:** There is nothing sacred about our bodies (transgenderism).
- **Answer:** A baby is not a real person until it is viable (abortion).
- **Answer:** God wouldn't want me to be trapped in a loveless marriage (divorce).
- **Answer:** Men and women should be equal in function (feminism).
- **Answer:** Some lives matter more than other lives (racism).
- **Answer:** Sex is necessary to live a fulfilled life (pre-marital sex).
- **Answer:** I have a right to decide whether I live or die (euthanasia).
- **Answer:** The poor are poor because the rich are rich (Socialism/Communism).
- **Answer:** The well-being of this earth is more important than the well-being of man (environmentalism).
- **Answer:** The earth is over-populated and must drastically reduce its numbers by millions or even billions.
- **Answer:** I can be anything I want to be.
- **Answer:** My actions have no bearing on anyone else.
- **Answer:** There is only one road I can take to accomplish God's will.
- **Answer:** There is no absolute truth.
- **Answer:** Sin does not exist.
- **Answer:** Individualism is a noble pursuit.
- **Answer:** Marriage is a social contract, and we have the right to define that contract.
- **Answer:** War is always immoral and never has any legitimate justification.
- **Answer:** There will be no final judgment.

Question 4:
- **Answer:** While resources such as the local newspaper and talk radio can be helpful in providing facts and educated opinions, these are usually divorced from a biblical understanding. As Christians, we should view all things firstly through a biblical worldview, not a partisan political perspective. We should be able to engage ideas from a familiarity with the Bible, not just a familiarity with the political talking points.

Question 5:

- **Answer:** Churches should be careful not to be so focused on being loving and accepting that they refuse to address culturally relevant issues.
- **Answer:** Churches should be careful not to be unnecessarily controversial, divisive, or demeaning in their defense of the truth.
- **Answer:** Churches should be careful not to lose sight of the gospel message in their effort to address culturally relevant issues.
- **Answer:** Churches should focus on teaching people biblical principles and how to be biblically-minded rather than tell people what they should believe about each issue.

Question 6:

- **Answer:** *Forerunners of America* provides researched materials on a variety of cultural subjects as well as web links to other helpful content and ministries (www.ForerunnersOfAmerica.org).
- **Answer:** President of Southern Theological Seminary Dr. Albert Mohler provides a blog and podcast call *The Briefing.* The podcast is a 20-minute daily analysis of news and current events from a Christian worldview (www.AlbertMohler.com).
- **Answer:** *Got Questions Ministries* offers an online database of evangelical answers to commonly asked questions. They have endeavored to answer approximately half a million Bible questions (www.GotQuestions.org).
- **Answer:** *Koinonia House* exists to create, develop, and distribute materials to stimulate, encourage, and facilitate serious study of the Bible as the inerrant Word of God. Koinonia House provides a radio broadcast, podcast, blog, weekly news updates, a monthly news journal, and seminary-level verse-by-verse book studies for the entire Bible, as well as numerous topical studies. They also host an annual Strategic Perspectives Conference focused on addressing geopolitical issues from a biblical perspective (www.KHouse.org).
- **Answer:** Dr. Michael S. Heiser is an author, an academic scholar, a professor of theology and biblical studies, and a scholar-in-residence for Logos Bible Software. He hosts several blogs and podcasts designed to minister to those whose experience has caused them to feel abandoned by their church because their spiritual leadership isn't intellectually equipped to help them or fears real interaction with the supernatural. The *Naked Bible Blog* and The *Naked Bible Podcast* address theological issues and provide exegetical teaching. The *Paleobabble Blog* critically evaluates archaeological and alternative history claims. The *UFO Religions Blog* critically evaluates claims from the UFO and extraterrestrial communities. The *Peeranormal Podcast* critically evaluates peer-reviewed journal articles on paranormal issues. And *Sitchin Is Wrong* refutes the claims of the ancient astronaut hypothesis, popularized in the writings of Zechariah Sitchin (www.DrMSH.com).
- **Answer:** Janet Parshall is an author, national speaker, and host of the Moody Radio programs *In the Market with Janet Parshall* and *Janet Parshall Commentary.* She offers observations on the news and current issues, endeavoring to reflect how a Christian should understand and approach such issues from a biblical perspective (www.MoodyRadio.org/Programs/Janet-Parshall-Commentary).

Question 7:

- **Answer:** We combat spiritual lies with the truth of God's Word in order to provoke conviction of heart and repentance. For those who are saved, this strengthens their faith and their relationship with God. For those who are not yet saved, our goal is to see the transforming power of the gospel free them from the power of the devil.
- **Answer:** Our primary goal should not be to change a person's political views.

Question 8:

- **Answer:** Maybe your relationships? Are you intentional about seizing opportunities to share the truth in your relationships? Are there opportunities to share with people you interact with but do not have a relationship with?
- **Answer:** Maybe your kitchen table or living room? Can you invite people to your house for games, dinner, or desert? Can you host a small group Bible study or discussion group?
- **Answer:** Maybe your church? Can you teach a Sunday school class? Can you be more intentional about your conversations in the hallways and fellowship areas of church?
- **Answer:** Maybe your mailbox? Can you mail newsletters, letters, or cards that inform, exhort, and encourage people in truth?
- **Answer:** Maybe your phone or computer? Can you use social media (Facebook, Twitter, Tumblr, etc.)? Can you use e-mail, text messages, phone calls, or a personal webpage? Can you start a blog or a podcast?
- **Answer:** The key is to look for natural opportunities to connect biblical principles with relevant issues. Often these will be mundane or routine elements of life that provide opportunities, not the obvious or provocative things.

Question 9:

Answer: Ephesians 4:15 teaches that we have an obligation to speak the truth, even if it causes offense. However, we should not be needlessly offensive or divisive. Instead, Ephesians 4:15 tells us to speak the truth in love. We are obligated to speak the truth, but we should do this in the most tender, yet meaningful, way possible.

Answer: People do not change unless they are first offended by their own behavior. In this sense, the truth should, and must, offend. If we are overly concerned about causing discomfort or offense, then we will likely never see change in the individual's life.

- **Answer:** Because Jesus loved people, He reached out to those whom society rejected as sinful reprobates; but He did not build relationships with sinners just to make them feel loved. Jesus was not afraid to offend sinners with the truth, after first demonstrating to them His genuine concern for their wellbeing. He never placed an individual's feelings above his need for salvation.

WILL YOU MINISTER IN POWER?
(LESSON 9)

Review:

Last time, we looked at not giving the enemy a foothold by understanding and walking in the truth. We also discussed taking new ground by identifying and confronting the lies of the enemy found throughout culture. These are often "hot issue" topics, and it is important that we stand firm on God's Word if we are to be effective ministers of the gospel.

Insight:

As children of God, we need not fear experiencing difficult times if God chooses to judge our nation. While no one wants to experience difficulties, it is often during times of trial and tribulation that God focuses and redirects His people and that the gospel is best spread. As such, a time of God's judgment could result in a great spiritual harvest of souls.

Question 1: Can God use tumultuous days in glorious ways? If so, how? Can you think of any current examples?

_____

_____

_____

_____

_____

_____

Question 2: According to Acts 8:1–5, how can tumultuous days and times of trial further the gospel?

_____

_____

_____

_____

_____

_____

Question 3: Philip could have become bitter over being compelled to leave his home and country because of his commitment to God. Instead, he preached Christ, and many people were saved. What do you think motivated him to preach Christ instead of becoming bitter?

_____

_____

_____

_____

_____

_____

Insight:

Tumultuous times can provide ample opportunity for Christians to contrast the culture and to take new ground for Christ, but this can only be effectively accomplished when we rely on the Holy Spirit. Until this point, our study has largely focused on the life of the mind—what we must know in order to stand strong and minister through difficult times. However, if we were to use the analogy of an airplane, the life of the mind would constitute only one wing of the plane. The other wing is life in the Spirit (Mark 12:18–27).

When we over-emphasize either the life of the mind or life in the Spirit, our lives and ministries become unbalanced. If one wing of the plane were longer than the other, it would become unbalanced and begin flying in circles. Likewise, when we over-emphasize knowledge and preparation, or when we over-emphasize God moving in power, we can quickly find our ministry efforts flying in circles (Mark 12:24).

Question 4: According to Acts 8:4–8, what was the result when Philip relied on the Holy Spirit in his ministry?

_____

_____

_____

_____

_____

_____

_____

Question 5: What can you accomplish when you rely on the Holy Spirit in your ministry?

_____

_____

_____

_____

_____

_____

Question 6: If we are promised such power in our ministries, why are we so often ineffective in our efforts for Jesus Christ today?

_____

_____

_____

_____

_____

_____

Question 7: According to Romans 8:5–6 and Galatians 5:16–17, what can you do to foster a relationship with the Holy Spirit where you are sensitive to His leading and to what He wants to accomplish through you?

_____

_____

_____

_____

_____

_____

_____

Insight for the Above Question:

Someone once asked the question, "If you have a white dog and a black dog, and you make them fight one another, how can you know which one will win?" This question was answered with another question, "Which one have you fed the most?" We know that the Holy Spirit and our sinful nature are in conflict with each other. Which of these are we feeding the most? Galatians 5:16–17 teaches that when we gratify the desires of the one, we necessarily weaken the influence the other has in our lives.

Before the era of digital radio, it was not uncommon for radio antennas to simultaneously receive signals from two separate stations. Generally neither station was particularly clear as they vied for dominance. When this happened, the radio dial would need to be slightly adjusted to retune to the preferred station. Once this adjustment was made and the signal was strong again, the other station could no longer be heard. The signal from that station was still being transmitted across the airwaves, but the strength of the other signal, combined with the fine tuning of the machine, prevented it from being heard. In some ways, this is the analogy the apostle Paul presents in Galatians 5:16–17. When we are tuned in to the Holy Spirit, we no longer hear many of the requests of our sinful nature. When we walk according to God's commands instead of according to our lusts and passions, we empower the Holy Spirit to lead us, and we have an increasing desire to be led by the Holy Spirit.

Question 8: How can you tune in to the voice of the Holy Spirit?

_____

_____

_____

_____

_____

_____

Question 9: How can you foster a meaningful prayer life?

_____

_____

_____

_____

_____

_____

_____

Insight:

If we wish to contrast the world and take new ground for Jesus Christ, we must rely on the Holy Spirit. This demands that we intentionally spend time in God's Word, guard our hearts and minds, walk by faith, and foster a meaningful prayer life.

Prayer Points:
- Ask God to grant you a heart that desires to see the gospel spread more than you desire comfort and peace.
- Ask God to protect you from becoming bitter over times of difficulty.
- Ask God to reveal to you those things which are interfering with your sensitivity to the Holy Spirit's prompting.
- Ask that your ministry would be filled with God's power.

Question 1:

- **Answer:** Adversity reminds us that God is present and we are accountable to Him for our every thought, word, and action. As the Institute for Basic Life Principles notes, God's Word reveals that the fear of the Lord is the key to life, wisdom, and lasting achievement (Proverbs 9:10; 14:27; 22:4). If we lose our awareness of God and begin to think and act as if He does not exist, He will often allow painful reminders of our need for Him—just as He did with the nation of Israel (**Judges 2:20–22**).

- **Answer:** God refines His people through times of difficulty, conforming their character and attitudes into that Jesus Christ (Dan. 11:32–35; Rom. 5:3–6; James 1:2–4). Sometimes this involves purging sin from among His people, and other times it involves strengthening their character and resolve. According to the Institute for Basic Life Principles, God uses adversity to:
  - motivate us to cry out to God (Psa. 34:17; 2 Chron. 7:13–14).
  - strengthen our hatred for sin (Gal. 6:7–8). In God's mercy, He exposes sin and allows others to see its devastating consequences. As we realize how sin keeps us from living in a way that honors God, and how it damages the lives of those we love, our hatred for evil increases.
  - expose pride (Prov. 11:2; 29:23).
  - purify our faith and develop patience (James 1:3; 1 Pet. 1:6–7).
  - cause us to desire more of Christ's power in our lives (Php. 3:8–10). Troubles reveal that, on our own, we can't live in a way that honors God.

- **Answer:** When times of adversity come, we are forced to face problems and pressures that are too big for us to resolve in our own strength. At these times, God is revealed as our provider, our strength, and our shield during times of difficulty (Psa. 18:1–3; 2 Cor. 12:7–10). When these qualities of God are on full display, they are powerful tools of evangelism.

  Answer: People are drawn to our hope when we are not afraid or discouraged by our circumstances, and this provides meaningful opportunities to share the gospel (1 Peter 3:14–15). When our attitudes and actions are righteous despite the circumstances, we shine like lights, contrasting the darkness of the world around us (Php. 2:14–15).

- **Answer:** God can use times of difficulty to mobilize His people and to spread the gospel message (Acts. 8:1–4).

- **Answer:** Over the last seventy years, God has used religious persecution in China to cause the church to grow exponentially.

- **Answer:** Over the last thirty-five years, in the face of dictatorial leadership, AIDS ravaging the population, and religious persecution, God has dramatically changed the country of Uganda. It is believed that as much as a third of Uganda is genuinely born again, and about two thirds of the population attend some kind of church service on Sunday mornings.

Question 2:

- **Answer:** God redirects Christians to new assignments.
- **Answer:** When we are comfortable, sometimes we become reluctant to go where God wants us. Discomfort can be a mobilizing force for God's people.

Question 3:

- **Answer:** He had a proper perspective. The trials of this life are temporary and fleeting in comparison to our future glory (Rom. 8:18; 2 Cor. 4:16–18).
- **Answer:** He had already weighed the cost of following Jesus. Philip served a Lord who had sacrificed everything for him and who had called him to be willing to sacrifice everything in return (Matt. 10:37–39).
- **Answer:** He cared about people. This is likely the same Philip who served as a deacon taking care of the needs of the neglected widows in Acts 6:1–7. Also, his choice to minister to the Samaritans reveals his concern for people. The Jews despised the Samaritans, but Philip refused to overlook them.
- **Answer:** He followed the leading of the Holy Spirit and relied on the power of God in his ministry (Acts 8:29–30).

Question 4:

- **Answer:** Philip brought the gospel to an unreached people group. The Samaritans were despised by Jews, but Philip reached out to them in love. Most likely, he chose to travel to Samaria when persecution struck Jerusalem because he was reminded of Jesus' instructions that through the power of the Holy Spirit, the gospel would be preached first in Jerusalem, then in Judea and Samaria, and then to the entire world
(Acts 1:8).
- **Answer:** The power of God was on full display when God used Philip to perform miracles. People were delivered from demonic oppression and healed of their physical disabilities and illnesses.
- **Answer:** The people were compelled to pay attention to what Philip was teaching.
- **Answer:** An entire city was influenced for Jesus Christ, and there was much joy in the city.

Question 5:

- **Answer:** When we are strengthened by the Holy Spirit in our inner being and allow Him to work through us, we can do far more than we can ask or think of. Many of us have wild imaginations, yet we are assured that we can exceed even our imaginings if we will truly rely on the power of the Holy Spirit rather than our own strength and understanding when we minister (Eph. 3:16–21).
- **Answer:** Jesus taught that when our faith and reliance is wholly on God, we can expect to do the works He did while on earth, and even greater works than those (John 14:12–17).
- **Answer:** When we place our faith and trust wholly in God's power and ability to work through us, we can accomplish anything (Matt. 17:18–20).

Question 6:

- **Answer:** Some of us do not truly believe the words we read in Matthew 17:18–20, John 14:12–17, and Ephesians 3:16–17. Some of us limit Jesus' words to the apostles and the early church. Others believe that Jesus was speaking figuratively and using exaggerated language to emphasize His point. Still others cannot accept the supernatural implications of taking Jesus' words at face value.

- **Answer:** Some of us are afraid of the supernatural. For some of us, inexplicable movements of God disrupt our comfort zones and remind us that we do not have the control over our own lives we'd like to believe. For others, we ignore 1 Corinthians 1:18, instead fearing the thought of being viewed as irrational by our peers.
- **Answer:** Some of us have too small an understanding of God. We have limited God to something we can fully comprehend and explain. However, an all-powerful and infinite God can never be contained within our finite minds. Until we are willing to allow God to be beyond our understanding and explanation, we will never fully witness His power.
- **Answer:** Some of us do not fully trust God and His Word. We are only willing to step out in faith so far before being held back by fear, our education, comforts, traditions, love for the things of this world, etc. In contrast, Hebrews 11 is known as the "Hall of Faith." It is filled with examples of people who demonstrated their faith in God by trusting Him and taking Him at His Word. As a result, they accomplished mighty works for God. However, if we are unwilling to risk everything in our devotion to God, we limit His ability to work through us.
- **Answer:** Some of us seek to receive credit for what God is accomplishing. Throughout the Bible, God worked His greatest feats through those who were evidently incapable of accomplishing such feats on their own. God will not give His glory to another (Isaiah 42:8). When we seek to exalt ourselves, we limit God's ability to work through us.
- **Answer:** Some of us are cherishing sin in our hearts (Psa. 66:18). We have not fully submitted ourselves to God and to the work He is accomplishing.

Question 7:

Answer: We can reject the desires of the flesh. These are described in Galatians 5:19–21 as consisting of sexual immorality, impurity, sensuality, idolatry, sorcery, enmity, strife, jealousy, fits of anger, rivalries, dissensions, divisions, envy, drunkenness, orgies, and things like these.
- **Answer:** We can learn what pleases God and follow after those things.
- **Answer:** We can focus our minds on the things that please God rather than things that please our flesh. This requires discipline regarding what we watch, listen to, imagine, hope for, fear, celebrate, etc. (Php. 4:8).

Question 8:

- **Answer:** We can read and memorize the Bible (Psa. 119:9–11). The Bible is God's Word. It reveals the heart and mind of God, and it teaches us how to please Him.
- **Answer:** We can surround ourselves with godly influences (Heb. 13:7). In Philippians 4:8–9, the apostle Paul encouraged the Philippian Christians to grow in their relationship with God by following the example of his life. Likewise, the Apostle Paul taught the Hebrew Christians to push and encourage each other toward love and good works (Heb. 10:24–25).
Answer: We can submit ourselves to those who have spiritual authority over us, such as our pastors (Heb. 13:17).
- **Answer:** We can respond quickly and in humble submission to the discipline of the Lord (Heb. 12:4–6).
- **Answer:** We can draw close to God in submission, and He will draw close to us (James 4:7–8).

- **Answer:** We can confess and repent of every sin God brings to mind (Acts 24:16; 1 Peter 1:14–16; 1 John 1:9).
- **Answer:** We can ask God for greater sensitivity to and reliance on the Holy Spirit (Luke 11:13; Eph. 5:18; 1 John 5:14–15).
- **Answer:** We can pray (Eph. 6:18). Every healthy relationship requires effective communication. When we pray, we are communicating with God. This builds our relationship with God, and it aligns our hearts with His. Pastor, missionary, and author Henry Blackaby has said, "We are filled with the Holy Spirit through prayer. When I get up from my knees, I am a different person than when I first went to prayer."

Question 9:
- **Answer:** We can devote a consistent period of time to concentrated prayer (Psa. 5:3; Luke 18:1–8).
- **Answer:** We can maintain a spirit that continually invites the Lord into our activities and seeks His counsel (1 Thess. 5:17).
- **Answer:** We can be thankful and express our gratitude to God (Php. 4:6).
- **Answer:** We can believe that God is listening to our prayers (Psa. 34:15; 1 John 5:14).
- **Answer:** We can believe that God desires to respond to our prayers (Matt. 21:22).
- **Answer:** We can understand that while God is not obligated to respond to our prayers, He is a merciful God who does hear and respond (Dan. 9:18).
- **Answer:** We can understand that unconfessed sin interferes with our prayers (Psa. 66:18). James 5:16 specifies that it is the prayers of those who live in righteousness that are powerful and effective. Likewise, Jesus specifies that it is those who abide in Him and in whom His words abide who will receive whatever they ask for in prayer (John 15:7).
- **Answer:** We can ask for things that align themselves with the heart of God rather than our personal desires (James 4:3).
- **Answer:** We can ask things of God boldly and with confidence (Heb. 4:16).
- **Answer:** We can submit our will and understanding to God, knowing that He knows best (Mark 9:24).

THE WAY FORWARD
(LESSON 10)

Review:

Over the course of this study, we've concluded that:

- nations play an important part in God's redemptive plan, and God's judgment of those nations includes both a destructive and a creative element. God designed nations to draw people back to Himself, and this remains the purpose for nations today.
- God uses national trouble to identify and distinguish the righteous from the wicked.
- America's relationship with God may be more precarious than we'd like to think. No nation is exempt from God's judgment if it sins.
- God does not choose sides. We choose to join God's side in faithful obedience to Him, or we choose to stand in opposition to God. God can both bless and curse any nation.
- America celebrates and flaunts the very sins for which God has judged nations in the past.
- America is likely experiencing corrective forms of judgment, and it is only God's mercy that is preventing a more severe form of His judgment. God's purpose for judging is not to crush a nation, but rather to redeem a people (2 Chron. 7:13–14).
- the church will not be exempt from judgment for national sins if the church is participating in those sins. As Christians, we are called to separate ourselves from worldly practices, ambitions, and attitudes (2 Cor. 6:14–7:1; Tit. 2:11–14; 1 John 2:15–17).
- if we wish to influence our nation for Christ, we must take new ground by speaking the truth with boldness. When we speak the truth, we draw a line in the sand and compel people to choose sides. Some may receive the truth and be grateful, but others will reject it and despise us for compelling them to choose and for shedding light on the spiritual lie that they have embraced (John 7:4; 2 Cor. 2:14–16).
- if we wish to influence our nation for Christ, then we must also minister in God's power (Acts 8:1–40).

Question 1: Reflecting on the first nine lessons, what should you do?

_____

_____

_____

_____

_____

_____

Insight:
God has designed our personalities, interests, and experiences to make us uniquely qualified to influence those around us. There are four key roles where you may specialize: watchman, intercessor, evangelist, coordinator. Each of these roles is important in accomplishing the greater vision of influencing those around us.

Question 2: According to Ezekiel 33:2-6, what does a watchman do?

_____

_____

_____

_____

_____

_____

_____

Insight:
A watchman is called by God to be vigilant, to discern the hour, and to spend time in His counsel in order to receive God's "now" message for His people and for our nation.
- He pays attention to what is happening in the culture.
- He knows how to identify and challenge the spiritual lies behind cultural ideas.
- He informs others of what is coming and how to think about these things in the way God does.
- He warns of the consequences of ignoring God's commands.

Question 3: What are some practical things a watchman might do?

_____

_____

_____

_____

_____

_____

_____

Question 4: According to **Ezekiel 22:29–30** and **Romans 8:26–27**, what does an intercessor do?

_____

_____

_____

_____

_____

_____

Insight:

An intercessor stands in the gap before God on behalf of the people and the land (**Eze. 22:29–30**).
-   He is a prayer warrior.
-   He asks God for mercy, justice, grace, and blessing on behalf of others.
-   He admits the faults of those for whom he is praying and asks God for forgiveness and forbearance (Dan. 9:1–21).

Question 5: What are some practical things an intercessor might do?

_____

_____

_____

_____

_____

Question 6: According to **Romans 1:15–16**, what does an evangelist do?

_____

_____

_____

_____

_____

_____

_____

Insight:

An evangelist shares God's message and seeks to apply the transforming power of the gospel to all things (Rom. 1:15–16).

- He boldly proclaims the ministry of Jesus Christ.
- He identifies sin and calls for repentance.
- He spreads God's message.
- He shows people how things could be through the power of the gospel.

Question 7: What are some practical things an evangelist might do?

_____

_____

_____

_____

_____

_____

_____

Question 8: According to Acts 9:26–27, what does a coordinator do?

_____

_____

_____

_____

_____

_____

_____

Insight:
A coordinator networks people and resources, uniting them together and organizing them into effective ministry.
- He finds and connects people of similar mind and purpose.
- He initiates conversations.
- He plan ahead, anticipating variables.
- He facilitates events to unite people of similar mind and purpose.
- He keeps people informed of important events and details.

Question 9: What are some practical things a coordinator might do?

_____

_____

_____

_____

_____

_____

Question 10: What are some practical things a coordinator might do?

_____

_____

_____

_____

_____

_____

Insight:
We are most effective when we work in community, where we can lean upon the strengths of others who are naturally bent toward the roles of watchman, intercessor, evangelist, or coordinator. In light of your desire to influence those around you and to help others be ready for whatever might come next to our nation, consider beginning a Forerunner Community Group.

Forerunner Community Groups regularly meet with others who are burdened for the nation. They generally meet in people's homes, and they meet to encourage, energize, and hold each other accountable. They also meet to help educate and prepare each other to stand firm and minister now and through difficult times.

Forerunner Community Groups:
- pray together. They serve as intercessors on behalf of their neighborhoods, churches, cities, and nation.
- strategize. They determine how to best influence their communities, both individually and as a team, and they serve as spiritual and cultural watchmen who warn the people and proclaim God's Word.
- evangelize. They seek out those who are spiritually lost, proclaim Jesus Christ, and share the gospel. They also demonstrate the transforming power of the gospel in all areas of life.

Question 11: What is your next step to influence those around you? What are your thoughts about beginning a Forerunner Community Group? Who might you invite to join you?

_____

_____

_____

_____

_____

_____

_____

Insight:
For further information, coaching, or training, visit www.ForerunnersOfAmerica.org.

Prayer Points:
- Having taken several weeks to discern the hour in our nation, take time to seek the Lord about what He wants you to do next.

Question 1:

- **Answer:** Discern the hour in which we live.
    - o Having strayed from God, America finds itself in a spiritual stupor.
    - o America is traversing a path destined for judgment.
    - o Nothing is holding back God's judgment against America except His grace and mercy.
- **Answer:** Repent.
    - o Before we as a nation can come to a place of repentance, the church must first repent of its complacency.
    - o We must repent of those areas where we have accepted spiritual lies and have joined the culture in its defiance of God's commands.
    - o We must repent from holding to the American dream, and turn instead to a kingdom of God lifestyle.
- **Answer:** Pray.
    - o Pray that Americans will awaken from their spiritual stupor.
    - o Pray that the church will be energized to share the truth of God's Word.
    - o Pray for mercy for our nation.
- **Answer:** Influence those around us.
    - o Alert people to the danger of forsaking God and disobeying His commandments.
    - o Encourage our Christian friends to speak the truth of God's Word with boldness
    - o Counter error with truth
    - o Share the gospel

Question 2:

- **Answer:** A watchman keeps his eyes fixed on the horizon, looking for danger, and he warns people of what is coming.
- **Answer:** A watchman discerns friend from foe. This can mean that he tests and discerns between the spirits, judging what is true and what is error (1 John 4:1).
- **Answer:** A watchman listens for what God wants to communicate to His people and shares it (Eze. 3:18–21).

Question 3:

- **Answer:** Ask his pastor if he can lead an adult Sunday school class to share what he believes God is saying to our nation and to challenge people to respond in faith.
- **Answer:** Speak to his small group.
- **Answer:** Ask his pastor if he can share his burden for our nation during a weekend service.
- **Answer:** Write a blog.
- **Answer:** Share this message on Facebook and other social media outlets.
- **Answer:** Have a dessert night or barbeque to share his concern for the nation with family, friends, and neighbors.

Answer: Be intentional in interactions with coworkers, associates, family, friends, and neighbors, seeking to capitalize on opportunities to share his message.
- **Answer:** Be prepared to provide specific details and offer practical advice and useful resources to those who have questions.
- **Answer:** Commit to hear God's voice for this day and hour.
- **Answer:** Learn God's standards and how to explain them using Scripture.

Question 4:
- **Answer:** An intercessor petitions on behalf of another.

Question 5:
- **Answer:** Make a commitment to regular personal prayer for the nation.
- **Answer:** Call other intercessors to regularly meet and pray together on behalf of friends, the workplace, the neighborhood, the church, the city, and the nation.
- **Answer:** Decide how often he will pray and where.
- **Answer:** Cry out for God's mercy.
- **Answer:** Pray for the lost.
- **Answer:** Learn God's heart by spending time in the Bible.

Question 6:
- **Answer:** Proclaims Jesus Christ as Lord and seeks to save the lost.
- **Answer:** Shares God's message.
- **Answer:** Applies the gospel to all areas of life.
- **Answer:** Draws attention to the transforming power of the gospel in people's lives.

Question 7:
- **Answer:** Reach out to his family, friends, neighbors, coworkers, and strangers in order to share his faith.
  Answer: Build relationships with those who need to experience the power of the gospel in their lives.
- **Answer:** Use social media and email to identify sin while also identifying how God wants to transform the situation.
- **Answer:** Train others how to share the gospel.
- **Answer:** Train others by inviting someone to go with him when he shares his faith.
- **Answer:** Disciple others, helping them connect their faith with their experiences and circumstances.
- **Answer:** Learn God's power by memorizing and meditating upon God's Word.

Question 8:
- **Answer:** A coordinator connects people together for the work of the ministry.
- **Answer:** A coordinator combines things and people so they work well together.
- **Answer:** A coordinator connects and arranges things in their proper position.
- **Answer:** A coordinator facilitates learning and ministry (Rom. 16:3–5; Col. 4:15).

Question 9:
- **Answer:** Facilitate events to unite people of similar mind and purpose.

- **Answer:** Schedule a potluck to bring together the watchmen, intercessors, and evangelists in his community to get to know each other.
- **Answer:** Choose a date and time to bring together the watchmen, intercessors, and evangelists in his community to seek God.
- **Answer:** Invite and arrange for a watchman to speak in his house or church.
- **Answer:** Contact people in his area to invite them to a gathering where a watchman is speaking.
- **Answer:** Organize a prayer chain.
- **Answer:** Organize a small group meeting in his home.
- **Answer:** Stay connected to other coordinators throughout his state and nation.
- **Answer:** Use email and social media to keep people informed of important events and details.

TEACHER'S GUIDE

AMERICA IN THE BALANCE

God's Perspective on
Nations and What to Do

ALSO AVAILABLE AS A TEACHING CURRICULUM!

Did you find *America in the Balance* helpful? Do you know others who might find it helpful? *America in the Balance* is available as a teaching curriculum for small groups and church Sunday schools. Moreover, it is specially designed to allow anyone to facilitate group discussion regardless of teaching experience, Bible knowledge, or familiarity with the subject. This may be the perfect tool to help you lead your friends through this content. It may also be ideal for your church small group or Sunday school programs. Download the teacher's guide and student notebooks for FREE at www.ForerunnersOfAmerica.org!

Made in the USA
Middletown, DE
12 December 2021

55388010R00049